The Lost Black Communities of Merrifield, The Pines and Williamstown

Marion Ransell Dobbins

The History Press

Published by The History Press
An imprint of Arcadia Publishing
Charleston, SC
www.historypress.com

First published 2025

Manufactured in the United States

ISBN 9781467159043

Library of Congress Control Number: 2025933738

CONTENTS

PREFACE

As a child, I sat on my grandma's knee in a place called the Pines. I listened for hours to her vivid memories of Jennie Williams, her grandmother. As the story goes, in 1844 Jennie was born enslaved in Fauquier County, Virginia. Like most people in bondage, she lived in a small log cabin at the slave quarters—a cabin with little to no nogging or insulation to stitch together the raw beams of wood placed to form primitive walls. When it rained, water rushed through the hued planks like a sieve and onto the dirt floor. The floor became muddy and caused most of Jennie's meager possessions to ruin. Grandma spoke of how my great-great-grandmother cooked in one large pot, a Dutch oven, and prepared meals after a long, hard day from sunrise to sunset, laboring for her enslaver. This is where my historical journey began.

My grandmother Myra Collins-Lee was born in 1902 to William Collins Jr. and Jennie's daughter, Betty Williams Collins. Myra lived most of her life on the land purchased by her father, William, who was a Buffalo Soldier and fought in the Spanish-American War. The homestead she grew up on, cultivated and later inherited was called the Pines—a segregated corner of Fairfax County, in the Providence District, where Black family farms clustered together, protected from racism, under the shadow of pine trees.

However, the Pines was but a small part of a larger community called Merrifield. In comparison, Merrifield was the hub of the area. It is where I was born and raised and where I worshiped, at the First Baptist Church of Merrifield. It is where I learned many life lessons on an acre of property

Above: A picture of the First Baptist Church of Merrifield, located on Ransell Road, Merrifield. The building was dedicated in 1966. *Courtesy of the First Baptist Church official website.*

Opposite: The Mosaic District in Merrifield, Virginia, a mixed-used development for retail, businesses and homes. It was built on land that was occupied by the Lee Highway Drive-In Theater and the Multi-Plex Cinema. *Courtesy of the Mosaic official website.*

my parents owned on Porter Road. Large walnut trees surrounded much of my neighborhood, where African American homesteaders, like my parents and I, lived.

Merrifield, or Mills-Crossroads, as it was called prior to the Civil War, was the beginning of decades of landownership for Blacks in the county. After the War Between the States and through Reconstruction, Freedmen purchased land and built homes, a church and schools, creating a safe space for their families. African American land purchasers in Mills-Crossroads assisted in

establishing other area communities, such as the Pines and Williamstown. As I look back, I find it devastating that the only material footprint left of these neighborhoods is the second church building. All other homes, shops and the 1894 original church structure are gone. Gone are the Liberty Lodge, Odd Fellows Hall, Household of Ruth and the IGA, a grocery store that also served as the Merrifield Post Office. Unfortunately, the landscape is now void of farmland and its small-town consciousness.

In contrast, the modern-day space is filled with condominiums, shopping malls, high-tech office complexes, a Target and a Pottery Barn—vastly different from its agrarian and segregated past. Cars have now replaced the horse-drawn wagons, and the ill-maintained, wooden corduroy roadways have been paved. In an oral history interview in August 1971, Ms. Pearl Dunn, a lifelong resident of Merrifield, described a corduroy road as "pine poles put down crossed laid in the road, this way and the men throwed dirt on it and usually as long as these big pine poles held out you had a pretty solid road."[1] Like the pine corduroy roads, the African American communities in Merrifield did not hold out and have been relegated to the back burner of history.

That historical back burner is the reason why I seek to offer a detailed account of the evolution and decline of the African American neighborhoods in the Providence District of Fairfax County. I want to emphasis the long-forgotten communities of Mills-Crossroads/Merrifield, the Pines and Williamstown. These are my neighborhoods, my old stomping grounds, where I lived and gained knowledge—places I held in high regard. They now exist solely in my collective memory as small spaces where Black families united via the First Baptist Church of Merrifield.

Equally important is the fact that few books have been written about these three areas, and those that are in print do not present a full, immersive experience of the communities and their people the way I do. The reason I am able to do so is I grew up in Merrifield, where thriving families of color worked and lived. I was raised near my grandparents' farm in the Pines and their home in Williamstown. Additionally, my research comes from listening to the elders or griots (keepers of the stories). Their oral histories have been passed down through the generations and gave me a firsthand glimpse of life within the borders of these places. I was born in Fairfax County, and I had a front-row seat to the demise of my hometown.

So, what happened to these neighborhoods? In the 1960s, the African American elders believe that Fairfax County systematically destroyed Black enclaves and wiped them from history. Many believe that the officials of the county used legal instruments, such as eminent domain or sanitation regulations, to dismantle these areas of Black culture. Because of this, I am here to give a voice to some of those lost, marginalized communities and their families, along with restoring their narrative back into the historical landscape of Fairfax, Virginia. I will never forget the impact these localities had on my life and the history of African Americans in the Providence District. After reading this book, you shall also know the history of these locations. This is why this book is so vital.

CHAPTER 1

ENSLAVEMENT

To begin, the Providence District, where Merrifield is located, was a slaveholding community. Enslavement of African American men, women and children in this region provided the free labor needed to sustain the well-being and financial stability of their enslavers. In the 1830s, the county of Fairfax was agrarian and rural, but after years of tobacco cultivation, the soil became depleted of the nutrients and minerals needed to grow crops. Because of this, land became inexpensive, and many northerners traveled to Fairfax in search of cheap property. With that, these northerners began the process of restoring the soil and revived farming in the area.[2]

Prior to the northern land grab, there resided a prominent white family in the Providence District called Chichester's. This family of farmers and millers also enslaved African Americans and lived in what would be called Mantua.[3] By 1778, Richard Chichester and his second wife, Sarah, had accumulated thousands of acres of land near Accotink and maintained it with their human property. Richard had a reputation for being demanding, and when he died, his son, Daniel McCarty Chichester, inherited some of the property. With his inherited land, Daniel built two mills along Accotink Creek, and by 1830, the mill was producing copious quantities of grain. As was the custom, when he passed away, his son, George, inherited portions of the land. George constructed a house and farm that he, or his father, named Mantua. When George died, his son from his first marriage, John Henry Chichester, maintained the farm with the help of his enslaved population. By 1850, John was listed as having sixteen enslaved people

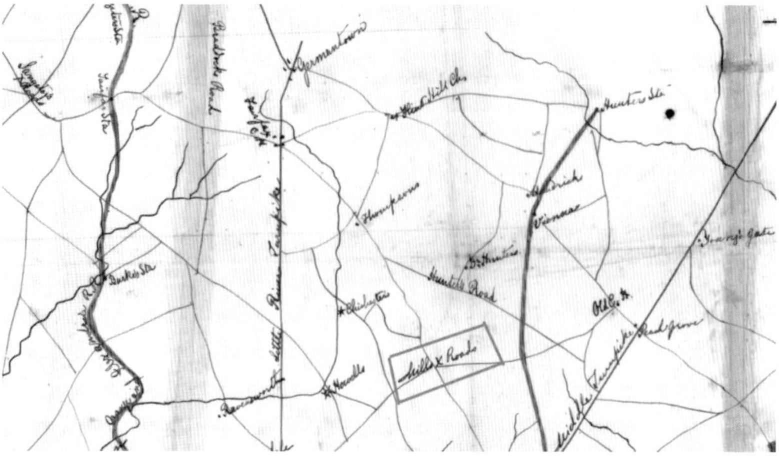

between the ages of two and sixty. John, along with the property of another relative, Jane Chichester, was close to Mills-Crossroads, and when war broke out, John had his enslaved laborers working his 548-acre farm. After the war, John Chichester found himself with new neighbors: Freedmen.

In 1860, the county had a total citizen population of 11,834, with a racial breakdown of 8,046 Whites (68 percent) and 3,788 Blacks (32 percent). An additional breakdown of the 3,788 African Americans shows that 3,116 of them were enslaved, with 672 being classified as free. When the war broke out between the North and the South, it was estimated that 4.5 million African Americans were enslaved in the rebellious Southern states. By 1970, the total number of White citizens had increased to 95.96 percent, and the Black population had dwindled to a mere 3.34 percent in the county. One can only wonder what caused such a drastic change in the African American population. I am still researching for answers; however, I also witnessed the exodus of my family, friends and churchgoers as they disseminated from place to place, spatially dividing to Arlington, Alexandra and even West Virginia—all to migrate away from Fairfax County.[4]

Stepping back into history with the book *The Quarters and the Fields*, Damian Pargas outlined the fact that "as Fairfax County planters adopted a system of diversified agriculture at the turn of the century, they in fact turned old plantations into mixed farms. Their slaves became jack-of-all-trades skilled in farm occupations from an early age."[5] Furthermore, Pargas stated, "The slave's workload in Northern Virginia increased during the nineteenth century as slave numbers dwindled due to hire or sale. This led to slaves working longer hours per day, and shorter periods of time off. Most enslaved people worked from sun-up till sundown, six days a week. Sunday

Opposite: The 1861 map of Mills-Crossroads, now known as Merrifield, in the Providence District of Fairfax County. Mills-Crossroads is highlighted near Chichester farm and Little River Turnpike. *Courtesy of the Library of Congress.*

Above: Photo of Chichester's millrace in Mantua, Providence District of Fairfax County. *Courtesy of Sue Kovach Shuman.*

is considered the enslaved 'time off' or freedom from their daily work, as it was labeled. However, the farm chores all ways take precedent."[6] Brendon Stevenson, a Northern Virginian historian, described the workflow of those enslaved in the county: "Their work was hard and often monotonous. Their workdays were long, and of leisure time there was precious little."[7]

In Eric Foner's book *Reconstruction: America's Unfinished Revolution, 1863–1877*, he stated, "Virginia's slave population was greater than any other state. By the 1860s there were over four million enslaved African Americans within the rebellious states of the Union. Most were illiterate and many suffered the trauma of witnessing family and friends being sold and sent to the Lower South's sugar cane or cotton plantations. Virginia, the first colony in British North America to provide slave labor from Africa in 1620, was now the state with the largest population of enslaved persons."[8] The driving force behind Northern Virginian's White prosperity was its unpaid Black labor force. However, through the death of planters and their heirs' inheritance, large plantations dwindled down to twenty- to thirty-acre farms. Even so, before the start of the Civil War, enslaved labor drove the economic engine of the Commonwealth both through agriculture and in acts of human trafficking, via breeding and selling slaves.

In 1863, the signing of the Emancipation Proclamation led to the abolishment of slavery in the rebellious states, transforming the status of enslaved individuals into that of Freedmen. This change affected Fairfax County, as Virginia was one of those rebellious states. Subsequently, formerly enslaved people in the Providence District found themselves free, and for these individuals, this newfound liberty sparked a revolution of independence and a strong desire to explore all aspects of life and liberty. It also marked the beginning of the Reconstruction era, during which formerly enslaved individuals became Freedmen and were given opportunities to purchase land next to former slaveholders. This situation was particularly evident in Mills-Crossroads.

The Reconstruction era was not a seamless transition and peaceful reconciliation; in fact, it was fraught with chaos, confusion and hardship. According to Foner, "All told, Reconstruction was the darkest page in the saga of American history."[9] History reveals that in 1865, Virginia, including Fairfax County, started the process of becoming reinstated into the Union. With the establishment of the Freedmen's Bureau in 1865 and the ratification of the Reconstruction Acts in 1867, Congress began the process of deciding what to do with these newly freed people of color.

Needless to say, Congress struggled to find a way to provide stability for these newly freed individuals, so those formerly enslaved thrived by establishing their own religious institutions, which also served as educational facilities. Freedmen purchased land, started businesses and built schools and churches. They raised their families alongside neighbors, many of whom had participated in the institution of slavery. Consequently, the initiatives taken by the Black community gave them a sense of agency within Fairfax and Mills-Crossroads. Their desire for equality and the American Dream drove African Americans to build a keen sense of community.

In his monograph *Lynching in the New South, Georgie and Virginia, 1880–1930*, W. Fitzhugh Brundage argued that landownership for Black Virginians helped to sidestep some of the labor issues that resulted in mob violence during Reconstruction: "Over the course of the late nineteenth century, substantial numbers of Blacks succeeded in buying land. The ownership of small plots of land, by itself, did not translate into economic autonomy, but it did provide much-valued independence."[10] He also argued that because of a diverse agricultural economy and landownership, Freedmen were not tied down to monocrops of cotton or tobacco, granting them a degree of autonomy. Landownership allowed the free people of color the independence to provide for their families, friends and communities. The

Photo of Freedmen's Village in Arlington, Virginia. Some of the soon-to-be residents of Mills-Crossroads and Gravel Bank lived there. *Courtesy of the Library of Congress.*

goal was to circumvent the financial tethering associated with White farmers through sharecropping or tenant farming, and because of this financial freedom, these landowners were able to create churches and schools to educate themselves and their families.

By the 1870s, as Reconstruction was ending, Freedmen in Northern Virginia were continuing the process of community building through land acquisition. Contractual agreements deeding farmland from Whites to Blacks placed African Americans in a unique position of sovereignty. Unlike sharecropping in the Deep South, proprietary rights in Northern Virginia allowed for self-sufficiency in farming and economic stability. Additionally, Black property owners would philanthropically bestow sections of land to the community for religious and educational purposes, giving African Americans in Northern Virginia additional pathways to prosperity. This ability to provide for the communities' religious and educational needs can be juxtaposed with those people of color living in the Lower South who were landless. In this region, through the establishment of these organizations, an era of literacy, community responsibility and personal empowerment, along with financial and economic growth, was ushered in. In other words, landownership generated agency and created useful civic and religious organizations for formerly enslaved people in Northern Virginia and Mills-Crossroads.

At the beginning of the 1880s, the African American community in Mills-Crossroads was growing as Blacks participated in a post-Reconstruction migration from Arlington, West Falls Church (Gravel Bank) and the "Hill" (Falls Church). Whites, such as Robert Porter, began selling parcels of land to people of color. Porter, who was born in the North and fought with the Union as an officer, was a large landowner in the Mills-Crossroads area. Deeds indicated that he sold land to African Americans, thereby giving them the opportunity to create permanent homes and farms in the Providence District. Another ex-military officer was a northern land speculator, Major O.E. Hine. Hine, born in New York, returned to the Merrifield-Vienna area around 1866 or 1867.[11] Upon his return, he began the process of acquiring large tracts of land. By 1878, as county records show, Hines owned 115 acres of land in Fairfax. By 1885, he had acquired wealth of more than $45,145, with a total of 6,440 acres of land in the county.[12] William Dunn was also a landowner in the vicinity. As a White merchant who owned a dry goods store at the main intersection of Lee Highway and Gallows Road, he serviced both White and Black customers at his mercantile establishment. Although Mills-Crossroads was a smaller community than its counterpart in Falls Church, it continued to grow in population into the 1900s, when the area known as the "Pines" was developed.

Likewise, to extend the radius of solidarity within the local Black congregations, religious leaders began to build church associations, such as the one that originated in 1877, the Northern Virginia Baptist Association

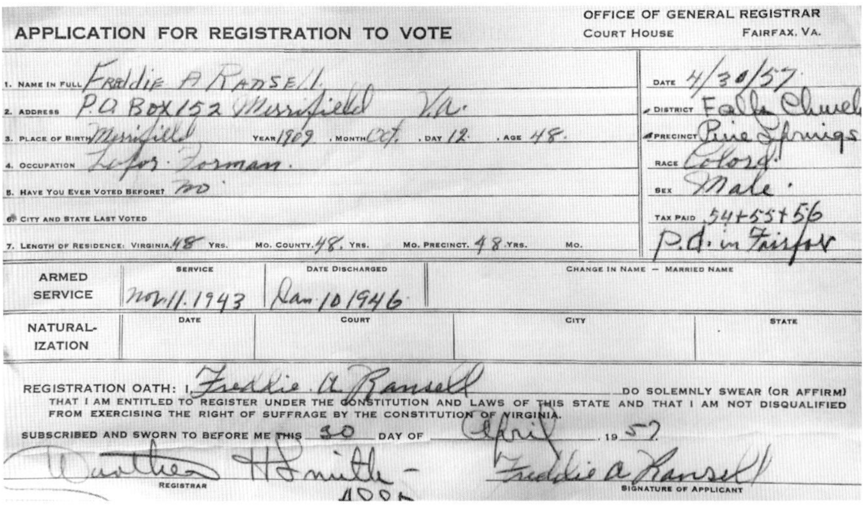

APPLICATION FOR REGISTRATION TO VOTE

OFFICE OF GENERAL REGISTRAR
COURT HOUSE FAIRFAX, VA.

1. NAME IN FULL Freddie A Ransell
2. ADDRESS P.O Box 152 Merrifield Va.
3. PLACE OF BIRTH Merrifield YEAR 1909 MONTH Oct. DAY 12 AGE 48
4. OCCUPATION Labor Foreman.
5. HAVE YOU EVER VOTED BEFORE? no
6. CITY AND STATE LAST VOTED
7. LENGTH OF RESIDENCE: VIRGINIA 48 YRS. MO. COUNTY 48 YRS. MO. PRECINCT 48 YRS. MO.

DATE 4/30/57
DISTRICT Falls Church
PRECINCT Pine Springs
RACE Colored
SEX Male
TAX PAID 54+55+56
P.d. in Fairfax

ARMED SERVICE — SERVICE Nov/11.1943 — DATE DISCHARGED Jan 10/1946

CHANGE IN NAME — MARRIED NAME

NATURALIZATION — DATE — COURT — CITY — STATE

REGISTRATION OATH: I, Freddie A Ransell DO SOLEMNLY SWEAR (OR AFFIRM) THAT I AM ENTITLED TO REGISTER UNDER THE CONSTITUTION AND LAWS OF THIS STATE AND THAT I AM NOT DISQUALIFIED FROM EXERCISING THE RIGHT OF SUFFRAGE BY THE CONSTITUTION OF VIRGINIA.

SUBSCRIBED AND SWORN TO BEFORE ME THIS 30 DAY OF April, 1957

Dorothea H Smith — REGISTRAR

Freddie A Ransell — SIGNATURE OF APPLICANT

Freddie A. Ransell's application for registration to vote in Fairfax County, April 30, 1957. The application shows that Freddie paid his poll tax for the years '54, '55 and '56. *Courtesy of author.*

(NVBA). Black religious and civic associations offered welfare assistance, contributed to missionary work, facilitated the construction of schools and churches and provided necessities for widows, orphans, retired ministers and students. A good example of assistance was families needing to bury their dead or help with financial aspects from illness or loss of a spouse. Additional hardships may have originated from legal problems through the inequality of justice. Furthermore, missionary work provided by African Americans to aid orphans, widows and the elderly was always in the forefront. Without the benefit of the community and associations, little assistance could be expected from the county, which was controlled by the White citizenry. Additional information on organizations and benevolent groups formed by Blacks in Mills-Crossroads will be discussed in later chapters.

Prosperity for Black individuals came with significant challenges as the early hopes of Reconstruction diminished. In the 1890s, the Jim Crow era emerged, and Fairfax County mirrored many other southern towns during this period. Like in the South, Fairfax was segregated, provided unequal educational opportunities for Black students, imposed a poll tax to restrict voting rights and enforced a separate but unequal society for African Americans. As the decades went by, simply owning land was no safeguard against the harsh realities of Jim Crow and its devastating impact on communities of color in Mills-Crossroads, the Pines and Williamstown. Nevertheless, despite the racial injustices, Black individuals in the area continued to grow their communities and neighborhoods, establishing deep roots of generational wealth that should have flourished for decades.

CHAPTER 2

MILLS-CROSSROADS/MERRIFIELD

Mills-Crossroads, also referred to as Mills-Crossings, was a deeply rooted Black community. It is now known as Merrifield. This small area, covering less than three square miles, is located within the Providence District of Fairfax County. It holds significant historical importance, particularly for some African American families in the area. History shows that Mills-Crossroads was a rustic village where farms, homes and businesses lined Gallows Road, situated between Arlington Boulevard (Route 50) and Lee Highway (Route 29). It served as a place where ordinary, working-class Black people bought homes, raised families, practiced their faith, watched over their neighbors and felt safe enough to not lock their doors. Additionally, Mills-Crossroads is the birthplace of two other African American communities: the Pines and Williamstown. Over the decades, this small section of the county has transitioned from rural homesteads to industrial complexes and has now evolved into a mixed-use commercial destination, featuring shopping and eateries.

To understand the history of this region, we must first look back to the eighteenth century. Prior to 1742, Fairfax County and Mills-Crossroads did not exist. Fairfax was established from land in Prince William County when, in 1742 the Virginia General Assembly enacted a decree separating portions of Prince William into Fairfax County. This legal action granted Fairfax its own legal jurisdiction, resulting in the creation of new land boundaries. Simply put, with a new legal jurisdiction, it made it easier for Fairfax residents to attend court closer to their homes to address legal matters. Coinciding with these new land boundaries, between 1742 and 1790 Fairfax had a growth spurt to nearly twelve thousand people, with 42 percent being enslaved.[13]

As Fairfax County's population increased, changes began to take place. By the mid-1800s, planters in Northern Virginia had shifted from growing tobacco to agrarian foodways. As history has shown, tobacco is a challenging crop to cultivate. It requires significant labor, depletes the soil of essential nutrients, degrades the land and makes it difficult for subsequent farming. Because of these factors, some planters in the area chose to leave Fairfax and move westward or deeper into the southern regions of the country. When they left, many planters took their enslaved workers with them, while others opted to sell them off.[14] Additional transformations occurred in the first half of the nineteenth century when northern Whites moved to the region, attracted by the milder climate and affordable land. These new landowners introduced different farming techniques, revitalizing the soil, which had been depleted by tobacco cultivation. These northern transplants applied lime, ashes and manure as fertilizers and implemented crop rotation, planted clover to enrich the soil and grazed their livestock, including sheep, cows and horses.[15]

As Prince William and Fairfax County continued its growth, planters shifted to a grain-based agrarian society focusing on staples such as corn and wheat crops.[16] Another shift was the subdivision of large plantations into smaller farms, primarily the result of plantation owners dying and leaving their vast land grants to be divided among their heirs. With inheritances creating a reduction of horticultural growing spaces, it also reduced the need for a large, enslaved workforce. This leads to an even greater transformation. With enslavers owning smaller farms and an excess of people in bondage, a new business emerged in Virginia: Human trafficking. Slaveholders found profit in their human property, selling individuals of color "down south" or renting them out to other farmers in need of workers or skilled artisans. A great majority of these (human) business transactions took place on New Year's Day. Unfortunately, history proves that Virginia was the largest slaveholding state in the Union.

In an article published in the *Fourth Estate* of 2015, Georgia Brown, an archivist for Fairfax County, noted, "When Virginia changed its agricultural system and cash crop from tobacco to grains, the demand for slave labor in the Commonwealth decreased, as the soil was left depleted from the tobacco. To continue making profit, Virginia slave owners started to export their slaves to southern states that grew cotton, like Alabama and Mississippi."

Photo of hogs in a pen at the Collins farm in 1949 in the Pines, Merrifield, Virginia. *Courtesy of author.*

Donald Sweig, the Fairfax County historian, surmised, "Some Fairfax County slaves, perhaps as many as 5,000, were sold to interstate slave traders in Alexandria and shipped to the deep south, to labor on the cotton and sugar plantations of Louisiana, Mississippi, and east Texas."

On nineteenth-century maps, the place called Mills-Crossroads appears, but to date there are no historical documents that definitively support who established the Crossroads or how. Some attribute the founding to a free African American man named Peyton Mills. For years, the story has been that Peyton operated a lumber mill at the junction of two roads, giving rise to the name Mill-Crossroads. But research provides a different story for Peyton. So far, there are no documents supporting the existence of a mill at the intersection of Lee Highway and Gallows Road. Additionally, there is no reference for Peyton Mills owning a mill. Further investigation shows that Peyton is listed in the 1850 census, but he is living as a free man in Stafford on a farm as a laborer. In 1864, he goes to Alexandria and marries Felicia Fookes, and by 1870, he and his wife are living in Vienna, Virginia. Later, he is listed in the 1880 census as a laborer and in the 1900 census as a farmer. The *Fairfax Herald* stated in 1900 that "Peyton Mills, a much-respected 'colored' neighbor, is in very ill health at present." Peyton Mills's death was recorded that same year.[17] Records show that Mills and his wife were laid to rest at the Liberty Lodge Cemetery in Vienna. Equally important is the fact that if Peyton was a free man of color, by law he would have needed to register as a "Free Negro" in the Free Negro Registry for Fairfax County. Peyton is not listed in the Fairfax records. Nor is he on the Personal Property Tax Ledger from 1866 to 1869. If he owned a mill during this time, his name and property would be listed on the ledger.

However, as previously stated, Daniel McCarty Chichester's mills were located close to the border of Mills-Crossroads. In 1801, Daniel applied for and received a mill seat on that property. Chichester's Mill, as it was named, was quite successful. Its most productive year yielded 4,500 bushels of flour. Chichester died in 1839, and the mill ceased operations after his death. Subsequently, in later years, more sawmills were established and operated by White individuals such as the Robeys and Dunns.[18]

It is a fact that mills were crucial in this region. Therefore, it can easily be surmised that the name Mills-Crossroads comes from Chichester's Mill, as Chichesters owned large swaths of land in the Providence District. Many old-timers say that the nickname for Mills-Crossroads was "Slabtown" because slabs of wood were manufactured by the mills for fuel to heat homes.[19] This story has been passed down through generations. However, there is controversy attached to the nickname. In a 1980 oral history statement, Everett Robey, a resident of the Providence District, said that the name Slabtown was because the slab road was made of wood.[20] As previously stated, the existence of the wood road was corroborated by Pearl Dunn, a lifelong resident.[21] Another question needs answering: Who owned the land that became known as Mills-Crossroads?

Property records noted on an 1860 map indicate that Margaret (Mary) C. Lee-Glassell, the widow of Charles Lee—the brother of Henry "Light-Horse Harry" Lee—owned the area later established as Mills-Crossroads. Glassell purchased two parcels of land totaling 403 acres. In 1835, she bought 253 acres for $1,500 and an additional 150 acres for $810 in 1837.[22] Margaret acquired these two parcels as part of the division of real estate from her late husband, Charles, to his children:

Fairfax County Map, showing Margaret (Mary) Glassell's 403 acres in the heart of Mills-Crossroads in the Providence District of Fairfax County. *Courtesy of Fairfax County History Commission.*

Alfred, Robert Eden and Elizabeth. As Charles's widow, and as specified in the deeds, this property was considered part of her marriage contract with Mr. John Glassell of Culpeper, Virginia. Adjacent white landowners to Glassell's property included Thurman Brush, Jane Chichester, Mary Chichester, Robert Darne, James Wren, Alexander F. Dulin and William Dulin. By 1860, Margaret C. Lee-Glassell was deceased, and the land was placed in a trust.[23]

Between 1840 and 1860, Fairfax County was a land-rich haven for people living in the North. Prices for land were low due to soil deprivation from tobacco growing. Land in the county was selling for less than a quarter of the price of land that was being purchased in the northern states. These newcomers from the north "planted wheat, not tobacco, and got good produce yields. They also rotated crops, planted clover to enrich the soil, and applied lime, ashes, and manure as fertilizer. Grazing cattle, sheep, and horses on a clover field rested the soil, while the clover and animal droppings enriched the land."[24] It goes without saying that the northerners brought new ideas and a fresh start to many of the abandoned farms in the county.

After the Civil War began, Lincoln drafted and signed the Emancipation Proclamation, providing freedom to those in bondage residing in the rebellious states beginning on the first day of January 1863. Because of this momentous decision, a new custom was established called the "watch

Photo of a 1960s "watch meeting" inside the original First Baptist Church of Merrifield, built in 1894. *Courtesy of Robert "Bobbi" Whitmore.*

meeting." The enslaved in the South watched from December 31, 1862, until January 1, 1863, for their freedom to materialize. To this day, First Baptist and many other Black churches in this county hold "watch meetings" to welcome in the New Year. When worshiping in the old church, I remember Freddie Ransell, Seth Williams and other men ringing the church bell, signifying the New Year's arrival.

After the turmoil and devastation of the Civil War, Northern Virginia began a restoration phase. However, it was different from the centuries that saw an all-White, male-dominated landscape. This time, it involved Whites and those who had previously been in bondage. After the conflict, land was decimated, and values in the county depreciated. This attracted more people from the North to purchase large parcels of land. Land was valued and sold as low as ten dollars per acre.[25] These lots were bought, subdivided and, in many cases, sold to Freedmen for profit.[26]

An excellent example is Frederick Foote, who purchased property in 1864 in Falls Church. "Foote bought 28 acres of land from Daniel Miner, who had once enslaved him—28+ acres of land now occupied by Koons, Eden Center, other Seven Corners businesses, apartments, and roads."[27] In some situations, Freedmen were given small plots of land by their former slave owners, or they found retired Union officers, now landowners and speculators, who would sell parcels of property to Blacks. People of color had several other reasons for wanting to purchase land and remain in the Northern Virginia area. One significant justification was to reunite with relatives who had been separated through enslavement. This area was the last home environment where these families had spent time together before being sold. With emancipation, there was optimism that those same family members could find their way back to their loved ones.

The southern states, after losing the war, sought admittance back into the Union, and Virginia was no different. In 1870, the state was readmitted, but this time boundaries were simply called the Northern and Southern Districts of Virginia. This division of the Commonwealth was done for tax purposes.[28] Research also sheds light on the fact that, by the 1870s, the Freedmen in Northern Virginia, and specifically Mills-Crossroads, were already acquiring their own land just a few short years after the Civil War. Simply put, these men and women once thought of and taxed as property were quickly becoming property owners themselves. The determination and forward thinking of formerly enslaved people in acquiring possessions assisted in their creating and binding families and communities together in short periods of time.

Additionally, freed Blacks living in Mills-Crossroads were listed within the volumes of Fairfax citizens who were taxed on land and horses, as well as material culture such as carriages, sewing machines and clocks. To understand the depth of these taxables, we can look at the work of Debbie Robinson with her research into Fairfax County's tax ledgers. Robinson's analysis of personal property taxes placed on African American men aged twenty-one and older is invaluable. Her data focuses on Northern Virginia after the Civil War from 1866 to 1868. Debbie notes, "The first-year former slaves appeared in the Fairfax County Personal Property Tax records was 1866. These records also detail the number and value of personal property items, such as horses, cattle, and watches."[29] She discovered that some former slaves listed on the ledgers were already residents of the county, while others had lived in Fairfax but had just reached the age of twenty-one. Another group consists of men who moved to the county after living in other parts of the Commonwealth.[30] Noteworthy names mentioned on the historical ledger include James and Charles Lee, who were born-free African Americans from Delaplane in Fauquier County, Virginia. The brothers came to Falls Church after the war, purchased land and assisted in creating schools, churches and an African American community. (More information on James and Charles is in the last chapter of this book.)

Reconstruction also saw the creation of the Freedmen's Bureau (or Bureau of Refugees, Freedmen and Abandoned Lands). The bureau, created in 1865, operated as a system to help shift the enslaved to a world of freedom. The bureau provided help with finding housing, food and medical aid along with establishing schools. It was also instrumental in legalizing marriages and finding sold family members. This federal operation was established in Fairfax County soon after the war ended in 1865. Equally importantly, Blacks in Mills-Crossroads were already becoming self-sufficient by the 1870s. They purchased land and farmed for food and profit through truck farming. These people of color-built homes for their families and a Baptist church, along with several benevolent orders. Most importantly, they would soon see their children enrolled in the "colored" schools to learn the letters and numbers that Virginia law had forbidden them from learning. Also, Blacks in Mills-Crossroads established organizations—such as the Sons and Daughters of Liberty Lodge, the Odd Fellows and the Household of Ruth—and had their own spaces or halls built within their own community. It is said that the Odd Fellows and Household of Ruth were noted for joining forces with the first NAACP chapter in the area, as this movement played a significant role in initiatives geared toward civil rights. The church and other organizations will be discussed in later chapters.

With the end of Reconstruction, Mills-Crossroads developed into a larger rural community, with both Black and White landowners. Today, the Merrifield area is more than just a landscape of two ethnic groups. It is a diversified population with a racial makeup of White, Black, Asian, Hispanic and others. It is an area of mixed-use developments, such as the Mosaic District. It is an affluent area with highly educated residents. Statistics provided by the 2020 U.S. Census Bureau give a glimpse into an area where 90 percent of residents have a high school diploma or better and 79.3 percent earned bachelor degrees.[31] This statistic is remarkable, as there was no high school for African Americans in Fairfax County or Merrifield until the opening of Luther Jackson High School in 1954, with its first graduating class in 1955. Prior to Luther Jackson, Black students in the Merrifield area were only offered schooling up to the seventh grade. My mother only had a seventh-grade education, gained by attending the same wooden, one-room schoolhouse her mother had attended. The school was across from First Baptist Church. In later years, students were bused twenty-three miles to Manassas Regional High School in Manassas, Virginia, for an academic diploma. More of this history is outlined in later chapters.

But where exactly did African Americans live in the Merrifield community? If you begin at the intersection of Lee Highway and Gallows Road and continue to the intersection of Arlington Boulevard and Gallows, you will follow the footprint of a once thriving Black neighborhood. I grew up within this space with my mother and father, Freddie and Eulala Ransell. There were also Blacks who lived on Hartland Road, about a half mile from the main intersection of Gallows and Lee Highway and continuing toward National Memorial Park Cemetery. In the '30s and '40s, this area near the cemetery was called Tremont. Tremont is also where the bus would pick up Black and White passengers going to or from Washington, D.C. My family would walk from the Pines to Tremont to catch the bus and walk the same route home.

Catching the bus from Tremont to Washington, D.C., was normal in Merrifield, and of course it was segregated. However, Gallows Road was also significant. The road has an interesting beginning. In the eighteenth century, it was once part of Alexandria Courthouse Road. This transportation route was used for traveling to and from Alexandria to the Fairfax County seat of government near Tysons Corner. In 1804, a new route was created called the Little River Turnpike, which led to Alexandria, Virginia.[32] Mills-Crossroads/Merrifield used Gallows Road as the demarcation line between the White and Black neighborhoods for decades. Figuratively, Gallows Road was an invisible border separating the races. Gallows was also a conduit between Lee Highway on one end and Arlington Boulevard on the other. Equally important is Interstate 495. Completed in 1964, the roadway stands in the backyard of Merrifield, parallel to Gallows Road. But for many, the issue that piques the curiosity of most is why Gallows Road was given that name.

Gallows Road

Fairfax County Librarian Elaine McHale said that people often come to the library seeking the origin of the name Gallows Road. Because of the public's interest, she created a document that explains that we know little about why the road has this name. "To understand this question better, we must return to the founding of Fairfax County. Once a part of Prince William County until 1742, the county built its first courthouse at the intersection of Ox Road and New Church Road (Route 7 and Route 123). However, in 1752, the court was taken to Alexandria. Even so, the name Old Courthouse Road lives on, which is near Tysons Corner."[33]

Elaine McHale goes on to say, "She found all sorts of interesting tales, including how residents were paid at the courthouse for each wolf they killed."[34] But she found not a single reference to a hanging at the original Fairfax Courthouse. Please note that the Fairfax County court did not hear murder cases involving White defendants. "Those cases were tried in Williamsburg, Va. It's possible that cases involving African American defendants were heard in Fairfax, and that they were put to death there, but no gallows is mentioned at the first court, though there is a mention of other punishments being meted out, including whipping and ear-cropping."[35] To understand the punishment of ear cropping, we look to the Historical Society of Pennsylvania in an article titled "A Quaint Colonial Custom":

> *"Ears Cut Off & Nailed to the Pillory!" Both in 1776 and in 1794, two slaves in Virginia, one for "running away from his master and lying," the other for "hog stealing," were ordered to be taken by the sheriff to the pillory, where their ears were nailed. The latter slave named Caleb, had one ear nailed, "and in one hour thereafter to cut it loose from the nail, then to nail the other and in another hour's time to cut that loose from the nail, this being the second offense."*

My mother, Eulala E. Lee-Ransell, born in 1922, hated walking Gallows Road at night, but not because of the tales of the gallows or ear cropping. Without a doubt, she thought the street was haunted. In the 1940s, Gallows Road was one lane, with both sides of the road from Arlington Boulevard/ Route 50 to the Pines lined with thick woods. There were long stretches of dense, dark tree canopies, and Eulala often said that the canopy was so heavy that during the day you had to pump in sunlight. She also said that when she and her siblings walked two miles from the church to home after attending a nighttime choir rehearsal, they could often hear footsteps and cowbells following them the entire way. Yet when they turned around to see who those steps or sounds belonged to, there was no one there. My mother said that it must have been the ghost of the prisoners walking to the gallows. After those experiences, she refused to walk Gallows Road at night. Eulala was not the only one who thought that Merrifield had apparitions and phantoms. Mr. Raphael Morales, who once ran the dry goods store in town, talked of haunted houses, a headless dog and more.[36]

Eulala E. Lee-Ransell. Photo taken at a voter registration event in Fairfax County, Virginia. *Courtesy of author.*

Some of Merrifield's history consists of folklore, much like the stories of Gallows Road. However, a great deal of information about the area is gleaned from oral histories obtained from residents living in this space during the nineteenth and twentieth centuries. One interview was conducted by Steven Matthews on August 20, 1971, with Mrs. Pearl Dunn, a lifelong resident of the Merrifield area. Mrs. Dunn, who is White, mentioned that her father, E.W. Dunn, owned the Dunn General Store at the corner of Gallows Road and Lee Highway.[37] Dunn states in the interview that her father's store was "nestled at the intersection of Lee Highway, then only a lane, and Gallows Road, also only a dirt road, said to have gotten its name because in colonial times miscreants were hung from gallows in stalls somewhere along the road. The best information I have been able to get is that Merrifield, originally known as Mill's Crossroads, was named after a freed slave who had built a small log cabin at the northeast corner of Dunn Loring Road and the dirt road that took you into Falls Church, three miles away toward Washington D.C.…[H]e was one of seven colored families who settled in this area immediately after the Civil War."[38]

As noted, records do not support the idea that a freed slave owned a mill in the area before the Civil War. Dunn went on to say that following the war, a northerner named Robert Porter, a retired second lieutenant from the Union army, acquired land in Mills-Crossroads. Porter, now a landowner, demonstrated inclusivity by selling property to African Americans. Some of the proceeds from Porter's land sales may have been used to support the White Merrifield school on Lee Highway, whose land deed stated that only White children could attend.

This historical context is further confirmed by the G.M. Hopkins map of 1894 for Fairfax County, which includes notations for both White and Black landownership, along with segregated area schools.[39] Robert Porter and other Whites in or near Mills-Crossroads—including E.W. Dunn, John Benson, Tobias Robey, Charles Taylor, Guy Humphrey, John Breniser, Charles Arnold and the absentee landlord J.W. Gaylord, with sixty-eight acres—interacted with Freedmen. So, the question remains: who created the Black community in Mills-Crossroads/Merrifield?

To understand the building blocks of the Mills-Crossroads African American community, you must look toward a retired White Union officer named Robert S. Porter. He was born on September 17, 1840, in Prattsville Green County, New York. He enlisted in the Union army in 1862 and retired as a second lieutenant. After the war, like many northerners, Porter seemed to become a land speculator and capitalized on purchasing land and selling it to Freedmen at a profit. Porter is listed as owning over $1,200 in real estate in 1870 while living in the Providence District and is listed as the landowner who sold lots to African Americans in Mills-Crossroads. In 1971, an article about Merrifield and Robert Porter was penned for the *Echoes of History*, a local periodical. After reading the article, Porter's son stated in a letter to the editor:

> *My father was a member of a Scottish family which settled in the Catskill Mountains of New York State prior to the Civil War. He enlisted in the Federal Army at the outbreak of the conflict at the cessation of hostilities he was the commanding officer of Company E 1311th New York infantry. Thereafter he came to Virginia and purchased…acres of land at the intersection of the Fairfax to Falls Church highway (now the Lee Highway) and the Gallows Road.…A fairly large number of northerners settled in the Mills X Road area.*[40]

The First Black Families of Mills-Crossroads/Merrifield

One area of investigation comes from the 1850 census. Mr. Charles Coates, born in 1809, is listed on the census as living in Alexandria, Virginia.[41] He was a born-free man of color and worked as a laborer. In the 1880 census, Charles Coates was listed as living in Fairfax's Providence District.[42] This is relevant because, in 1850, Mr. Coates had a son, John Coates. Charles's son was one of the earliest African American residents in Merrifield. John was listed on the G.M. Hopkins 1894 map as living on five acres of land at Mills-Crossroads. John was also listed, in 1892 and 1894, as a trustee for the land acquisition to establish the First Baptist Church of Merrifield.

Equally important is Mr. Nimrod Dixon, who purchased land, along with Joshua Ball, who bought property in 1876.[43] Both acquired the properties from Robert Porter and are listed as trustees for the Merrifield Colored Church. It's interesting to note that in 1866 Dixon rented twenty-eight acres in Alexandria from the Bureau of Refugees, Freedmen and Abandoned Lands for seventy-five dollars per year. Nimrod farmed his land, and after the rental fee was paid, he was allowed to keep the proceeds. The money from his proceeds may have been used to buy the land in Mills-Crossroads. Furthermore, Horace Gibson, a blacksmith in Ilda, Virginia, purchased land from Porter in 1878, and his son, Wesley, obtained the property before moving to Washington, D.C.[44]

In later decades, Horace's grandson Clarence Gibson owned land in Merrifield and was the first Sunday school superintendent I remember for the church. On his death certificate, he was listed as a welder and machinist

Photo taken in the late '40s or early '50s of the pastors and leaders at the First Baptist Church of Merrifield while worshiping in the original church. *From left to right*: Deacon Freddie A. Ransell, Deacon and Sunday School Superintendent Clarence Gibson, Reverend Charles L. Parker, Samuel or Chester Pearson, Reverend Eugene Terry and Vernand Ransell. *Courtesy of author.*

who also owned his own business in the District of Columbia. I vividly remember Mr. Gibson. He was a soft-spoken and devoted member of the church. However, he did have a brother we called Uncle Boogie. To my knowledge, Uncle Boogie didn't attend the church. But I would see him crossing Gallows Road with his dog, seemingly quite inebriated. In contrast, Clarence Gibson was a successful businessman with a son, Allen Gibson, who was a retired officer in the U.S. military and later a deacon at the church. Other Black residents who became early landowners in Merrifield were Robert Bradley and Joshua Pearson in 1884.

Robert Bradley, a prolific realtor, purchased land from Robert Porter and then divided the property into plots and sold them to his fellow Freedmen.[45] In 1892, he sold a piece of land for one dollar to establish the First Baptist Colored Church in Merrifield. On the deed, the original trustees are listed as Joshua Ball, Joshua Pearson[46] and John Coates. Unfortunately, the deed had one stipulation: the church could never use the property for burials.

To the church's dismay, in 1892, it was discovered that Bradley lacked a clear title from Robert Porter to sell the property.[47] Consequently, in 1894, a

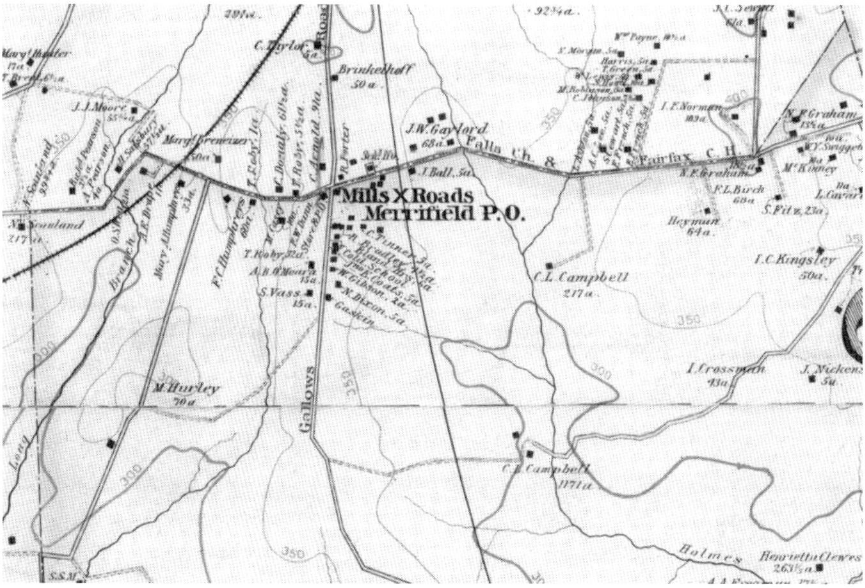

A Hopkins map from 1898 showing Mills Crossroads, Merrifield Post Office and the African American landowners Joshua Ball, Charles Tinner, Robert Bradley, George Bland, John E. Coates, Wesley Gibson, Nimrod Dixon and George Gaskin. The "Colored School" is also shown. *Courtesy of the Library of Congress.*

new deed was drafted and updated with additional trustees—John Coates, Joshua Ball, Joshua Pearson, William Steward and A. Dixon—for an agreed-on sum of five dollars. Moreover, the congregation of the church is believed to have been organized early in the 1870s, following the settlement of Freedmen in Mills-Crossroads and the Gravel Bank.

By 1894, there were other landowners in Mills-Crossroads, such as Mr. Charles Harrison Tinner, owning five acres of land; Robert Bradley, four and a half acres; and George Bland, six acres. Next to Bland is the Merrifield Colored School House. Then there is John E. Coats with five acres, Wesley Gibson with two acres and Nimrod Dixon with five acres of land. With these property acquisitions, the Black farmers were well on their way to achieving the American Dream through a means of landownership and truck farming. Truck farming involves growing copious quantities of produce, such as vegetables, to sell or ship to other markets, and in this case, it was K Street, or Georgetown, in Washington, D.C. These farmers not only grew crops to feed their families but also harvested extra produce to take to the commercial markets.[48]

Who, then, are the founders of Mills-Crossroads? Based on information from land deeds, census records and oral histories, it is believed that the seven African American families residing in Mills-Crossroads by 1894 and mentioned by Pearl Dunn were Joshua Ball, Charles Tinner, Robert Bradley, George Bland, John E. Coats, Wesly Gibson and Nimrod Dixon.

THE GRAVEL BANK

Many who lived in Mills-Crossroads first found themselves living in "Gravel Bank," a neighborhood aligned with the train tracks and Railroad Avenue, off Shreve Road in Falls Church, Virginia. This space was once a robust area of African American families, homes and businesses. The founder of this community was a Black woman named Lucinda Gaskins.[49]

In 1865, as the Civil War ended, Gaskins purchased land for seventy-five dollars because of its proximity to the railroad. The railroad—initially named the Alexandria, Loudoun & Hampshire Railroad but later renamed the Washington & Old Dominion Line—attracted other Black residents to the area and was nicknamed the Gravel Bank. The availability of job opportunities related to the railroad, specifically in moving freight to and from Broad Street and the West Falls Church station, motivated Blacks to relocate to the area. In addition to housing, other amenities such as a barbershop, shoe repair and a store were established. Both Black and White residents supported these businesses.[50]

The Gravel Bank area in Fairfax County experienced an influx of Black settlers attracted by work opportunities and places to live. One notable figure was William H. Collins Sr., who originally lived in the Bank but later moved to "the Pines" in 1905 with his son, William H. Collins Jr. In fact, William H. Collins Sr.'s brother, Thomas Collins, was also documented living in Gravel Bank during the 1870 census. Tom later married Lucinda Gaskins's daughter, Elizabeth. Thomas and Elizabeth had a daughter in May 1873 and named her Lucinda after her grandmother. Upon Elizabeth's mother's passing, she inherited a portion of the land. Notably, the Gravel Bank area remained under the ownership of descendants of Lucinda Gaskins and other families—including the Tinners, Whitneys and Rectors—until the early 2000s. Thomas Collins died in 1917 and is buried at the Second Baptist Church, Falls Church cemetery.

Spanish-American War Comes to Merrifield

Additional transformation within this agrarian hamlet was seen when the sword of war started rattling. The cry from many Americans was "Remember the *Maine*."[51] On February 15, 1898, in a Havana harbor, a U.S. vessel named the *Maine* was sunk, with 268 American soldiers losing their lives.[52] The blame was placed on Spain, and the incident was the catalyst for the Spanish-American War. In the buildup to the conflict, the need to train troops became vital. The area chosen to establish a training camp was the Falls Church area of Dunn Loring in Merrifield, Virginia. In the middle of the conflict, Merrifield citizens found themselves surrounded by twenty-three thousand soldiers from sixteen states.[53]

Those soldiers found themselves in a rural county a few miles from the nation's capital. On May 3, 1898, a training camp called Camp Alger was built. Alger was named after the secretary of war, and his support for the training area was the reason behind the designation. However, due to a typhoid outbreak and other unsavory conditions, the camp was decommissioned in August of the same year.[54] Camp Alger was described as:

> *Located 7 miles from Washington, D.C., 5 miles from Fort Myer and 1½ miles from the Dunn Loring train station on the Washington, Ohio and Western railroad. The surface of this tract is rolling, partly wooded, with cultivated clearings and with good drainage. The soil is made of clay and sand and nearly impervious to water. Immediately after the selection of this camp preparations*

> *were made for the reception of troops by the erection of storehouses at Dunn Loring, where the Southern Railway put in extra sidings to accommodate the increased traffic. It was built on a 1,400-acre farm called Woodburn Manor.*[55]

Writing home in 1898, Private George B. Thayler, Company K, First Connecticut, stated:

> *As we are camped on a treeless, thirty-acre lot, covered with weeds and corn stubble and two inches of fine dust, you can better imagine how utterly useless it is for us to keep clean.…Everyone comes back from drills covered with sweat and dust, mixed together.…I like this camp, for it is comparatively free of bad rum and mean women.…I also like the rough experience here, for it is the nearest to the real thing we have seen.*

Another Black community close to Merrifield was Ilda. The Ilda community had direct ties to Camp Alger. Viola and Doris Johnson grew up in Ilda, which was located a mile from the Pines, off Woodburn Road and Little River Turnpike. Viola and Doris's grandmother was born and enslaved in Goochland, Virginia. Her name was Katherine Johnson. Katherine was a mulatto because her father, Peter Lacy, was White and her mother was enslaved. At the end of the Civil War, Katherine, in search of a better life, did not stay in Goochland. She ventured north to the Providence District. When the Spanish-American War broke out, she provided laundry service for the soldiers at Camp Alger. Viola, in her oral history, said that her grandmother made five dollars per week and saved most of it. When she had saved up enough money, Katherine purchased thirty acres of land in Ilda for ten dollars per acre.

Settling into her land in Ilda, Katherine Johnson had ten kids, and one was Viola's father, Walter Johnson. Viola spoke of learning a good work ethic from her life in Ilda and Merrifield. She and the other children did chores on the farm from sunup until sundown. She said that her family was working to become somebody, and because of this philosophy, they never asked anyone for anything. They had dairy cows and pigs, churned their own butter and sold chickens. There was also hog-killing time in October. Her family would kill ten hogs, and once preserved, the pork meat would last them through the winter. One of the family's main sources of income was truck farming, growing produce and selling at the markets in Washington, D.C. She learned other valuable lessons, such as cold packing vegetables, which is a form of canning. Her family preserved apples and peaches by drying the pieces on a scaffold, like the practices of Native Americans in preserving meat and other products.

Even after the Civil War, despite the fact that Black men fought so bravely Black citizens in Merrifield, Ilda and the surrounding areas had to vote in semi-secrecy. Viola said it was not safe to talk about voting or encouraging your African American neighbors and family members to vote. If her father, Walter, wanted to talk to folks about politics and their rights, he never came out and said it directly. He camouflaged the activity as just regular decisions or meetings. She went on to say that you voted in silence because "her father called Fairfax 'Cracker Town,' and the whites did not like Black people."[56]

There is truth to the notion of racism in the county. As I researched old newspaper articles, I found a quote in the *Fairfax Herald* of a KKK cross burning near a farm in Merrifield: "A cross was burned by the K.K.K. near Willowmere farm, on Lee Highway near Merrifield, Monday night last."[57] But there are several stories that never made the *Fairfax Herald*'s newsroom. Freddie Ransell talked about the night the KKK attempted to burn a cross in the Pines. Fortunately, local Black men met the white-robed cowards with shotguns and told them to never come back to burn a cross again. Another story was about Freddie's mother, Jennie Ransell. Jennie was doing housekeeping in her home in the Pines when a knock came at the door. She opened the door, and there stood a White man. He told Jennie he was looking for a "Nigger" to take care of his kids. Jennie excused herself, returning several minutes later with a handgun. She instructed the man to get off her property and never come back. He heeded her advice, left and never returned. I have no idea how the African Americans in Merrifield were comfortable enough to challenge the White establishment so brazenly. I like to think it is because the Black community was woven together so tightly that when racism tried to slip through the threads, Black people knew they had one another's backs.

The White Side of Things

In the 1890s, Mills-Crossroads had a diverse but segregated population. Whites lived on one side of Gallows Road, while Blacks occupied the other side. During this time, Mills-Crossroads was primarily agrarian for both ethnic groups. The landowners farmed typical crops and raised animals conducive to a rural lifestyle. Ironically, decades later, despite this area being only ten miles from the nation's capital, land values had depreciated, making it inexpensive to buy. In the 1960s, the combination of low real estate prices and proximity to the capital created an ideal opportunity for land speculators to purchase property from African Americans. This process ultimately led to the dismantling of the Black community known as Merrifield.

But not all the Whites were born or raised in the Fairfax area. Several individuals came from outside the United States, from as far away as Germany and Puerto Rico. People from these other regions purchased land and started raising their families in Mills-Crossroads just as the northerners did. One prominent figure in the Merrifield community was Raphael Morales, a native of Puerto Rico. At the corner of Gallows and Lee Highway, Morales owned a one-room store, equipped with a post office. In 1893, he sold the store to Mr. E.M. Dunn, who was Pearl Dunn's father. Mr. Dunn continued to operate the post office and expanded the store. Following the Spanish-American War in 1898, Raphael and his family decided to leave Mills-Crossroads and relocate to Cuba. In the 1900s, Raphael's son, William Henry, established the National Bank of Cuba, which became one of the largest American banks overseas. Sadly, in the 1920s, Mr. Dunn passed away, and the store he purchased from Mr. Morales was sold.[58]

In the 1870s, as the community grew, the need for a White school became evident. The White community organized the Mills-Crossroads Literary Society. J.W. Gaylord, Robert Porter's brother-in-law provided the community with a plot of land, "sixty-six by one hundred forty-two feet, for a school building." There was a stipulation: the school was for education and religious purposes and for White children only. If any of these conditions were breached, the land would revert to Gaylord or his heirs.[59]

On October 8, 1874, the following citizens held land in trust for the all-White Merrifield School: Robert S. Porter, Charles Arnold, Tobias Robey, John C. Brenizer and John Darne. These five original trustees were often referred to as the White founding fathers of Merrifield by the old-timers. Ms. Dunn mentioned attending the second schoolhouse, built in 1898 on the footprint of the first school, which was built in 1874. She then attended the all-White Falls Church High School for three years. It was a segregated institution for learning that students attended for three years, but the school was never accredited. The first and second primitive White schools in Merrifield were situated on the grounds of the current Merrifield Community Center, next to the Merrifield Garden complex. Behind the red brick community center is a Whites-only cemetery where Ms. Dunn's relatives, along with Mr. and Mrs. Robert Porter's bodies, are interred.

Ms. Dunn went on to say that her father's store was not the only establishment in Merrifield. She said there was another store across from Dunn's Grocery.

Ada and Jack Walker first owned the business. Pearl stated in her interview that Ada was a Robey before her marriage to Mr. Walker. She also stated that Mr. and Mrs. Walker would never "look the Dunns' way" or even speak to them in passing.[60] She found this quite odd, as Ada was one of the founding families of Mills-Crossroads. Shortly thereafter, Mr. Walker died, and his wife sold the store. The new owners never made their business as profitable as the Dunns, with the property changed hands multiple times. Pearl Dunn also stated that one owner allowed Black people to hold Lodge meetings in the upper level of the store. This could have been the beginning of the Sons and Daughters of Liberty Lodge.[61] She went on to remember her father

> *Only made a half cent a pound on sugar and you'd have to weigh it and furnish the scales to weigh it and paper bag and tie it up…with string for half a cent a pound, a cent on two pounds of sugar. I'd grind the coffee and put up the sugar in two pounds and five-pound bundles. Got ready for our usual Saturday rush, always had a Saturday rush coming in.*[62]

Unlike today, with the Tysons Corner complex of hundreds of stores, the folks in Merrifield shopped at Dunn's general store. This dry goods establishment sold everything from needles to gloves, underwear, socks, handkerchiefs and lace. But after Mr. Dunn's passing, Mr. Isaac Vincent purchased the general store and continued the postal services.[63] Helen Haight, a lifelong Black resident of the Pines and the Merrifield area, recounted in an oral history how Vincent's store was a place frequented for ice cream after choir rehearsal. Helen reminisced about First Baptist Church of Merrifield located less than a block away, making it convenient to walk to the corner of Gallows Road and Lee Highway for a chilly treat. Mr. Vincent

Photo of Vincent's Store at the intersection of Lee Highway (Route 29 directly in front of store) and Gallows Road on the left-hand side of building. *Courtesy of Fairfax County.*

was quite the entrepreneur. He had registered several trade names in Fairfax County by the 1940s: Vincent's Diner and Vincent's Luncheon Room, along with Vincent's Hardware and Mercantile Store and Vincent's Garage and Service Station. It is assumed that the last two trade names were for one establishment, the one located in Merrifield. Further research should be done. Avonjeanette Lee-Hill stated that while in Vincent's store, you could not pick out merchandise on your own. You had to tell the shopkeeper what you wanted or hand him a list, and then he would collect the items for you to purchase. One would think this treatment would negate any fond memories of the store and getting ice cream after choir practice.[64]

In addition, there were other businesses that were not friendly to Helen and her family because of their race. The only restaurant in town was Harvey's Restaurant, later named Harvey's Hickory House.[65] It was located across the street from Vincent's store and was established in 1946 as a retail merchant, restaurant and tobacco shop. Needless to say, it was also segregated. Harvey's eatery refused to serve Black customers unless they went to the back door to order their hamburgers. Nonetheless, Harvey's had Black employees doing the dishes and cooking the meals. One of the cooks was Ms. Bessie Mae Gaskins; everyone loved Ms. Gaskin's cooking, and everyone loved Ms. Bessie Mae.

I knew Ms. Gaskins very well. She was a spiritual hero, a warrior for Christ. Her claim to fame was her voice. Ms. Gaskins would come to church, and someone would ask her to sing a solo. Bessie Mae would come to the piano, lift her chin toward the ceiling and present a sound of pure tone and clarity. I loved to hear her sing as she reminded me of Mahalia Jackson. Her voice was robust and forceful yet sweet and calming at the same time. She was also a Deaconess at the church. Women in the church who were Deaconesses were highly respected and had great poise and dignity. I can only imagine the treatment she received at Harvey's. It is astonishing to learn that in the communities of Mills-Crossroads and the Pines, African American customers were unfairly targeted due to an unjust policy based on unfounded fears of theft. Most African American families in Merrifield were landowners who cultivated their own produce to sell in the markets of Georgetown and D.C. These individuals were self-sufficient, devout and law-abiding. They had no need to resort to stealing. They already owned homes, built a church, established benevolent associations, grew their food and established a staunch support network within their Black community.

Another prominent White family who lived in Merrifield on Lee Highway were the Seoanes. John Seoane came to Fairfax County from Lugo, Spain, via

Photo of the Gospel Messenger Chorus. The image was taken during its anniversary service at the First Baptist Church of Merrifield. Second from the left in the first room is Deaconess Edith Collins-Terry. Second row, third from the left, is Ruth Johnson, and next to her is Bea Terry. Third row, second from left, are Trustee James Johnson, Aaron Terry and Lillie Gaskin-Morarity. Last on the back row is Deaconess Bessie Mae Gaskins. *Courtesy of Robert "Bobbi" Whitmore.*

Puerto Rico around 1875.[66] While in Puerto Rico, he met his bride, Cornelia Hulderman. In the 1890s, John and Cornelia moved to Merrifield, where they purchased a farm and raised their children. In the 1960s, the Seoanes moved to another part of the county but still maintained ownership of their Merrifield property. Interestingly, as soon as the Seoanes left Merrifield, a new, uninvited occupant took residence on their land. His name was Clay Cook, a World War II veteran from Washington, D.C. Without permission, Clay built a small cabin that lacked plumbing and electricity onto the Seoanes' property. He lived there, undisturbed, for several years. It was not uncommon

Seoane family farmhouse. *Courtesy of Fairfax County Library Photo Archive.*

to see his laundry drying on a clothesline or a table sitting outside with a tablecloth. While Mr. Cook could be considered homeless, he managed to create a homestead on the old Seoane farm. When the original farmhouse was torn down in 1971 Cook's cabin also met the same fate. With several pushes from the bulldozer, both Seoane's farmhouse and Clay's cabin were gone. Whatever happened to Clay is unknown. What is left to memory is that Mr. Cook never harmed anyone. He just needed a place to call home. Later, in the 1970s, Robert Seoane, the son of John, developed property next to his family's original home at the corner of Lee Highway and Gallows Road. Robert constructed the Merrifield Plaza equipped with a grocery store, pool hall, restaurant, ice cream store, laundry mat and a Dart Drug Store.

Charles Arnold was another White veteran who arrived in Merrifield prior to the Civil War. Arnold was born in Württemberg, Germany, in 1847 and immigrated to the United States. Arnold joined the Union army on June 21, 1864. After the war, he married Armenta J. Arnold in 1868 and applied for a war pension. A native of New York, Arnold purchased around twenty acres of land in Merrifield when property values were at their lowest. After purchasing a large swath of acreage, he quickly became a farmer and painter. Arnold, Pearl Dunn's grandfather, is recognized as having sold land for one dollar to build Bruen Chapel.[67]

Another iconic landmark from the twentieth century was located at the corner of Lee Highway and Gallows Road. It was impossible to miss because it was much more than an auto shop—it was the Johnston's Auto Paint and Body Works.[68] Since 1963, Mr. Edward Johnston owned and operated the body shop. Over the years, he decorated the exterior of the building with collected antique bits and pieces, German-style window boxes, a working water well and pictures hand-painted on the outside by a local artist named Kena Ruffner.[69] The shop was a talking point for the community. I know because I lived near the auto body establishment. I saw this delightful folk art building every day. Unfortunately, Mr. Johnston got older and so did the building. It fell into disrepair and was demolished in the early 2000s. It is now a vacant lot at the edge of a shopping center, next to a fast-food restaurant.

With the many changes to Merrifield over the decades, we look at men who were not from Virginia, like John Seoane from Spain, Charles Arnold from Germany, Guy Humphrey from Connecticut, Rafael Morles from Puerto Rico, Robert Porter from New York and John Brenizer, from Pennsylvania, as some of the White founders of Mills-Crossroads. Another individual who did not live in the Crossroads neighborhood but purchased a large amount of property was J.W Gaylord. Mr. Gaylord was a land speculator from New York, and with his brother-in-Law, Robert Porter, they purchased copious amounts of acres within the Providence District.

Johnston's auto body shop. *Courtesy of Fairfax County Library Photo Archive.*

THE HOMESTEADS

The homesteads of Merrifield date back to the 1870s and continued until 1985, when the last resident, Freddie Ransell, sold his property on Porter Road. Deciphering the locations of structures and residences of the Black families in Merrifield during the '30s and '40s is made possible through the collective memory of Avonjeanette Lee-Hill and the U.S. Census. Mrs. Hill, a remarkable community historian, has extensively documented the area's history and outlined the segregated spaces within the community. She recalls many of the families living in the Merrifield area—Charles Harrison Tinner, Henry Bland, Isaac Clinkett, Clarence Gibson, Stanley Turner, John Coates, William Jones, Phillip Luckett and William Johnson. At the corner of Porter and Gallows Road was Everett and Edith Terry. Next to the Terry's was the Original First Baptist Church of Merrifield. On the opposite side of Porter Road was where Liberty Lodge once stood. This space is now occupied by the Silver Diner. Next to the Lodge lived William Blackwell, followed by Jessie Terry, John Woodland, Irving Washington, Robert Johnson, Joseph Collins (William Collins Jr.'s brother), Harvey Bates and Harry Ward. The Merrifield Colored School was also on Porter Road, and the site is now the parking lot for a hotel.

Other African Americans came to the neighborhood. Freddie Ransell and Roscoe Collins moved from the Pines to Merrifield, and behind what is now the McDonald's on Gallows Road lived Mr. George Hyson and Reverend Norman Howard. It was also the site of the Second Colored School, built in 1939. Others who lived in the area included Chester Pearson, Walter Hyson, Charles Hyson, Charles Jackson, Brock Wells, James Whitmore and many others.

To provide more context to the community, in October of 2007, Ms. Aileen Wright, Gladys Parker's daughter, who was Moses Parker's granddaughter, gave an oral history account of life in Merrifield. Aileen's ancestor Moses Parker was the partner of a blacksmith shop with Horace Gibson. Gibson, a founder of a Black community called Ilda, also purchased land in Mills-Crossroads. Alieen recounted that only two White families lived on the other side of Gallows Road, the families of Mr. Anderson and Mr. Robey.[70] The opposite side was where the African Americans of Merrifield lived. Robey's farm across the road had fields of watercress. Alieen recalled picking watercress from Mr. Robey's fields. She also remembered Gallows Road being tar topped, which provided a smooth surface for roller skating. She enjoyed skating on Gallows Road, going down the hill from the site of the current McDonald's to Route 29, Lee Highway.[71] This was a remarkable experience, as the modern-day traffic congestion would not provide a safe place to roller skate. Aileen and her sister lived in Merrifield with her godparents, Annie and Joseph Collins, after her mother and father passed away. To connect the dots, Joseph Collins was the brother of William Collins Jr., who lived in the Pines. Joseph was also the brother of Norman Collins, Aileen's father, who was tragically murdered on Christmas Day.

The Merrifield Post Office

After Morales sold the store to E.W. Dunn, Mills-Crossroads experienced another change. In 1881, the name Mills-Crossroads was officially retired and changed to Merrifield. The new name was derived from the last name of a prominent resident in the Falls Church area, G.A.L. Merrifield. Merrifield arrived in Northern Virginia in the 1870s.[72] As with other northern transplants, G.A.L. was in search of cheap land and enjoyed the milder Virginia temperatures. Merrifield also held the position of postmaster, along with being an employee of the Pension Bureau of the federal government. "He was also a trustee of the Falls Church Congregational Church and a treasurer of the Oakwood cemetery."[73] G.A.L. was also an active member of the Whites-only Merrifield Improvement Association. On April 12, 1890, the post office at Merrifield was certified "for the establishment of an [official] Post Office in Fairfax."[74] Avonjeanette remembered that postal mail for the Pines was delivered to Vincent's store. She and her siblings were tasked to go to the store and collect the family's mail. She mentioned this was done after she had completed her studies at the Merrifield Colored School. She also felt the people in charge were not accommodating toward Blacks, but this was the only way they received postal services for the Pines.

As time passed, the Vincent and Dunn's stores were no longer in operation, leaving a food void for people living in the area. Fortunately for the residents, next to the footprint of those businesses was the IGA grocery store. IGA stood for Independent Grocery Association, and between the years of 1957 and 1959, ten new IGA stores were opened in Northern Virginia—Merrifield's IGA was one of them.[75] Similar to the Dunn and Vincent stores, the IGA also housed the Merrifield Post Office. In the mid-1960s, stepping inside the IGA and heading back toward the post office placed you back in time. In my mind, I still envision a dusty lunch counter on one side of the wall of the store. Alongside the lunch counter, divided by a partition, stood the Merrifield Post Office. The counter and display cases were filled

Photo taken in the 2000s of the old Independent Grocery Assocation (IGA) building, which had been converted into a Mattress Discounters store. IGA was located next to the old Vincent store at the intersection of Lee Highway (Route 29) and Gallows Road. *Photo taken by author.*

with unpurchased merchandise that seemed eerie. Containers of candy necklaces, candy cigarettes and empty cake display containers were visible.

The mailroom was always poorly lit, with dark, brown-colored walls. The official P.O. boxes, arranged by numbers, stood along one side of the partitions, dividing the store from the post office. The postmistress, Ms. Davis, was busy at work and would only lift her head and speak over her wire-rimmed glasses when spoken to. She was a petite White woman who sat behind a little window with bars. She was incredibly quiet and polite and seemed a little timid. My mother was fond of Ms. Davis. Our family's P.O. box number was 152, and the absence of postal delivery in our Black neighborhood meant that we had to make the half-mile trip to the IGA to collect our mail. In an oral history interview given by my neighbor Robert (Bobbi) Whitmore in 2021, he stated that his father was one of the first Black mail carriers in Falls Church. This position allowed his family a comfortable living.[76] I remember Bobbi and his father, and I was amazed that a Black man could be a mail carrier. He was the only one I had seen in my area as a child. He truly was an anomaly.

The folks who managed the Merrifield IGA store were extremely kind to me. One employee always gave me an orange popsicle that tasted like it was made in heaven. The store was small but efficiently laid out, except for the dilapidated lunch counter. The store faced Lee Highway, near the intersection of Lee and Gallows Road. It was situated near the old Vincent store that had been torn down before I was born. During my time in the 1960s, Black people could go into the IGA, pick what they needed off the shelf or go to the butcher and ask for meat, which was carefully wrapped in brown paper and tied with twine. In my day, there was no list to hand to the shopkeeper or someone collecting our groceries for us. Yet ironically, since the COVID epidemic of 2020, it seems that we have reset to the older ways of shopping. Shoppers place their orders, and clerks or store employees gather items from the store shelves and place them into the back of our vehicles. The old IGA building still stands close to the intersection of Gallows and Lee Highway. It has morphed into several businesses over the years, including a mattress discount store, and now the building is for sale or lease. When the IGA shut down, Mr. Sloane's son, constructed the Merrifield Plaza, at the corner of Lee Highway and Gallows Road. The two anchor stores were the A&P Grocery Store and Dart Drug. Also, to my pleasure, there was Carvel ice cream, where a large cone was only fifty-two cents.

Wartime

Many Black men from the community answered the call from their nation. Several Merrifield and Pines residents were World War I veterans. Norman Collins and Avon Lee were two of them. Avon Lee was the husband of Myra Collins-Lee. Seth Williams, from Williamstown, was a World War II veteran, along with others from the area who fought, including Freddie Ransell, Vernon Lee and Everett Terry. There were other African American

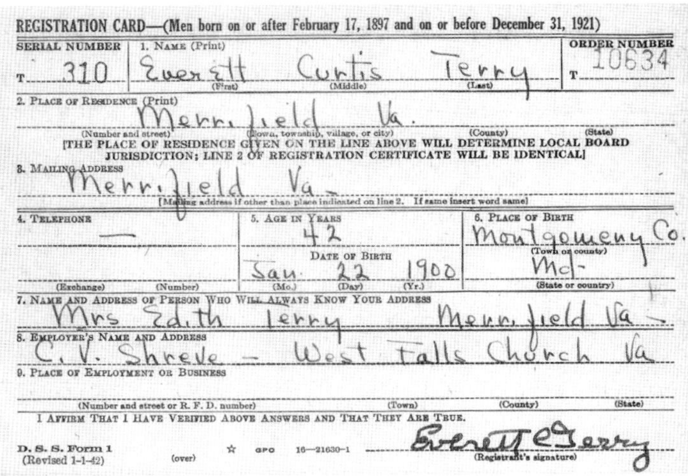
REGISTRATION CARD—(Men born on or after February 17, 1897 and on or before December 31, 1921)

SERIAL NUMBER T 310 | 1. NAME (Print) Everett Curtis Terry (First) (Middle) (Last) | ORDER NUMBER T 10634

2. PLACE OF RESIDENCE (Print) Merrifield Va.
(Number and street) (Town, township, village, or city) (County) (State)
[THE PLACE OF RESIDENCE GIVEN ON THE LINE ABOVE WILL DETERMINE LOCAL BOARD JURISDICTION; LINE 2 OF REGISTRATION CERTIFICATE WILL BE IDENTICAL]

3. MAILING ADDRESS Merrifield Va.
[Mailing address if other than place indicated on line 2. If same insert word same]

4. TELEPHONE — (Exchange) (Number) | 5. AGE IN YEARS 42 DATE OF BIRTH Jan. 22 1900 (Mo.) (Day) (Yr.) | 6. PLACE OF BIRTH Montgomery Co. (Town or county) Md. (State or country)

7. NAME AND ADDRESS OF PERSON WHO WILL ALWAYS KNOW YOUR ADDRESS Mrs Edith Terry Merrifield Va.

8. EMPLOYER'S NAME AND ADDRESS C. V. Shreve – West Falls Church Va.

9. PLACE OF EMPLOYMENT OR BUSINESS
(Number and street or R. F. D. number) (Town) (County) (State)

I AFFIRM THAT I HAVE VERIFIED ABOVE ANSWERS AND THAT THEY ARE TRUE.

D. S. S. Form 1 (Revised 1-1-42) (over) ☆ GPO 16—21630-1 Everett C Terry (Registrant's signature)

Registration card of Everett Curtis Terry for purposes of a draft in World War II. *Photo obtained from Ancestry.com.*

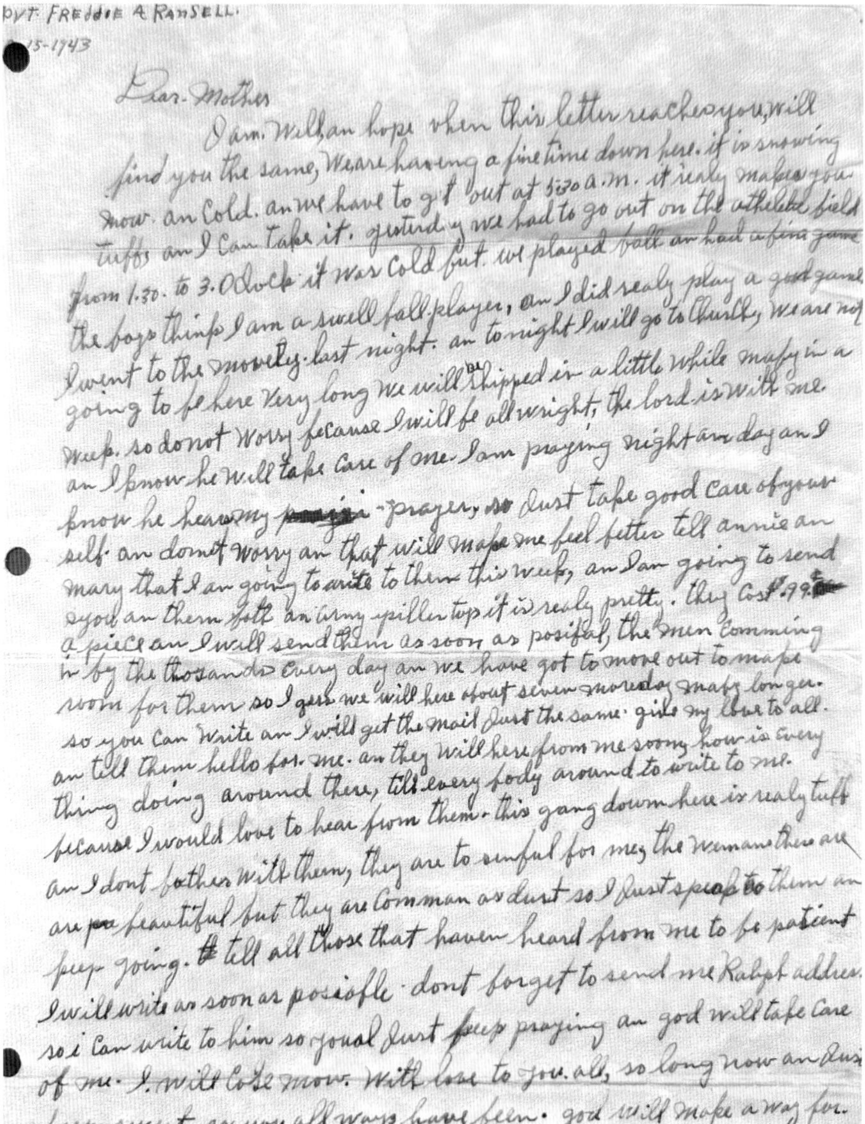

PVT. FREDDIE A RANSELL.
15-1943

Dear-Mother
I am well, an hope when this letter reaches you, will
find you the same, We are having a fine time down here. it is snowing
snow. an Cold. an we have to get out at 5:30 a.m. it realy makes you
tuffs an I Can take it. yesterday we had to go out on the athletic field
from 1.30. to 3. O'clock it was Cold but we played ball an had a fine game
the boys thinks I am a swell ball player, an I did realy play a good game
I went to the movely last night. an tonight I will go to Church, we are not
going to be here very long we will be shipped in a little while maby in a
week. so donot worry because I will be all wright, the lord is with me.
an I know he will take care of me. I am praying night an day an I
know he hears my ~~prayers~~ prayers, so Just take good care of your
self. an dont worry an that will make me feel better tell annie an
mary that I am going to write to them this week, an I am going to send
you an them both an army piller top it is realy pretty. they cost .99¢
a piece an I will send them as soon as posibal, the men comming
in by the thousands every day an we have got to move out to make
room for them so I gess we will here about seven more day maby longer.
so you can write an I will get the mail Just the same. give my love to all.
an tell them hello for me. an they will here from me soon. how is every
thing doing around there, tell every body around to write to me.
because I would love to hear from them. this gang down here is realy tuff
an I dont bother with them, they are to sinful for me, the womans there are
are beautiful but they are Comman as dust so I Just speak to them an
keep going. tell all those that haven heard from me to be patient
I will write as soon as possible. dont forget to send me Ralph address
so i Can write to him so you all Just keep praying an god will take care
of me. I will Close now. with love to you. all, so long now an Just
keep sweet. as you all ways have been. god will make a way for.

Above: Letter written by Private Freddie A. Ransell in 1943 to his mother, Jennie Ransell, providing an update on his well-being while serving in World War II. *Document courtesy of author.*

Opposite: U.S. Civil War soldiers record for John Ransell, Freddie Ransell's grandfather, who served in the U.S. Colored Infantry and is now part of the African American Civil War Memorial. *Photo obtained from Ancestry.com.*

ancestry.com

U.S. Civil War Soldiers, 1861-1865

Name:	**John Ransell**
Side:	Union
Regiment State/Origin:	U.S. Colored Troops
Regiment Name:	2 U.S. Col'd. Infantry
Regiment Name Expanded:	2nd Regiment, United States Colored Infantry
Company:	D
Rank In:	Private
Rank In Expanded:	Private
Rank Out:	Private
Rank Out Expanded:	Private
Film Number:	M589 roll 71
Memorial:	Part of the African American Civil War Memorial
Plaque Number:	A-6
Displayed As:	John Ransell

Source Information:
National Park Service. *U.S. Civil War Soldiers, 1861-1865* [database on-line]. Provo, UT, USA: Ancestry.com Operations Inc, 2007.
Original data: National Park Service, Civil War Soldiers and Sailors System, online <>, acquired 2007.

Description:
This database contains the names of approximately 6.3 million soldiers who served in the American Civil War. In addition to their names, information that may be listed for each soldier includes regiment, company, and rank.

men who fought but are not listed in this book. The war was a hardship for both Black people and White. War knows no color, and times were hard, with rationing of food, clothes and gasoline.

Freddie Ransell, a World War II veteran, was born in 1908 and raised in the Pines. He attended the First Baptist Church of Merrifield, where his mother, Jennie Collins-Ransell, served as the organist after becoming a widow. During his time in boot camp, Freddie frequently wrote letters to his mother, providing insight into their relationship, which was shaped by the challenges of war, segregation and genuine mother-son love.

Freddie's father, William Ransell, passed away when Freddie was a teenager. William was born in 1860 into slavery and was listed on a slave schedule, indicating that his mother was named Rachel from Mecklenburg, Virginia. Following his father's death, Freddie became involved in the family's farming routines and was responsible for delivering produce to the Washington, D.C., markets using horse and wagon. This task was a recurring duty during the holiday season. Freddie would chop down eight- to nine-foot pine trees and haul them to Washington, D.C.'s wealthiest residents to sell as Christmas trees.

During the war, Freddie served as a carpenter. He completed the seventh grade at a one-room schoolhouse in Merrifield and excelled in mathematics. As a child, he dreamed of becoming an engineer and building things. Unfortunately, due to segregation and unequal educational opportunities, he never had the chance to pursue an advanced degree. Nevertheless, before the war, he worked for Waverly Taylor, a man who built swimming pools for the elite on Foxhall Road in Washington, D.C. This experience provided him with a skill set for constructing anything, including the house I grew up in and the church where we worshipped. Freddie was not the first in his family to fight. His grandfather John Ransell, born a slave, served in the U.S. Colored Troops, 2nd U.S. Colored Infantry, in the Civil War. His name is enshrined at the African American Civil War Memorial in Washington, D.C.

Summer nights on our front porch, Freddie would recount some of the harrowing experiences of World War II. He vividly described landing on the Normandy beachhead on D-Day+1, where he witnessed the surreal sight of a beach stained red with blood. He shared accounts of narrowly escaping enemy shell attacks aimed at the ammunition depots he had constructed. Coping with the stress of war, Freddie found solace in writing reassuring letters to his mother, promising her that he would return home soon and unharmed. Amid the grim realities of war, he also fondly reminisced about the baseball games he participated in during his military training. He acknowledged that his fellow soldiers recognized his skills as a gifted baseball player. Like many African American men in Northern Virginia, Freddie had honed his baseball prowess through years of playing sandlot baseball.

Ms. Carey Johnson, a Black woman, was a proud owner of property in Merrifield, just off Porter Road. For years, Ms. Johnson graciously allowed the Black community to utilize some of her land as a baseball field. Over time, this area has transformed into a bustling mecca for office buildings and Yorktown apartment buildings. Avonjeanette recounted that prior to the war, on sunny weekends, numerous African Americans from the area would gather to enjoy spirited baseball games on Ms. Johnson's fields. During one game, Freddie bravely stopped a line drive, despite breaking four of his fingers. His dedication to the game was truly inspiring, as he refused to stop

Depicted is Hazel Lee-Moss holding the water pump handle, as well as her cousin Evelyn standing beside her. *Courtesy of author.*

playing until the game concluded. Baseball was a cherished pastime for the Black men of Merrifield and the surrounding area, and the women were always there to provide their enthusiastic support.

While Freddie and others were at war, both my mother and her sister Avonjeanette Lee-Hill remembered how they endured rationing of gasoline and sugar but, worst of all, silk stockings to win the war. Thank goodness food was not an issue. Both women claimed to have enough provisions for the family. Through it all, my mother made it clear that the people of the Merrifield community helped one another. If someone was in need, their neighbors or family members would help. It didn't matter about your skin color. Mom said that her family helped many White families who were in need.

On the homefront, my mother was also aware of the Double-V program. African Americans in Merrifield and those enlisted were aware they were fighting for victory on two fronts: the victory against fascism and the victory against Jim Crow. Black men were fighting Germany and Japan, yet on their own homefronts, they still needed to fight against segregation and struggled toward securing full civil rights. Lapel pins were created with a Double-V and worn proudly by those who understood the cause. Historians have noted that the infancy of the civil rights movement was birthed by the African American men returning from World War II, where they witnessed people liberated from German occupation who treated the Black soldiers with respect and dignity. Many of the Europeans looked on Black soldiers as liberators, not as second-class U.S. military personnel.

The awareness of the Europeans appreciation and profound thankfulness sparked a fire in the returning Black warriors' bellies. If they fought for Europe's freedom, it was time to fight for theirs. My father, after the war, worked at Fort Myer, an army post in Arlington, Virginia, for more than thirty years. However, until Truman desegregated the Armed Forces, the post was a military installation of separate and unequal. Bathrooms, water fountains and eating halls were separated by the color of your skin. Freddie told me one day that the commander of the post spoke with the Black working civilians. Freddie told the commander, "I went overseas to fight Hitler, and I must use the Colored toilet only." With Executive Order No. 9981, President Truman desegregated the U.S. military and its installations in 1948.

During World War II, my mother's sister Myra worked in the main cafeteria at the Pentagon in Arlington Virginia. Myra was a beautiful, light-skinned woman with gorgeous brown hair and a figure to match. One day, the supervisor for the women who worked in the officer's mess hall came to Myra and said that the Generals Dining Hall needed a light-skinned Black woman to serve the generals and upper-level officers. She was immediately assigned to the dining hall, where Dwight Eisenhower was having supper. After her shift, Eisenhower told the supervisor of the facility to have Myra as the permanent wait staff for his dining hall.[77]

She went on to serve other high-ranking officers and celebrities, such as Lana Turner and Clark Cable. My mother, who worked the night shift at Arlington Hall's mess, told me one night that James Cagney came to get a bite to eat. She cautiously asked him if he was Cagney. He stated that he was Cagney's cousin. My mother knew better.

Avonjeannette, in an oral history interview, spoke of her family's winter food preparation while living in the Pines before, during and after war:

> *They canned. And I hated the cellar; I hated canning time because I was young and afraid of dark holes. They didn't have a basement like we did; it was a hole dug under the ground under your house, and it was a cellar, all this was wood, it was cold down there it was just like a refrigerator or a freezer. And my grandfather cut shelves into the earth, and they put wood on top of it to put your vegetables and stuff on, but it was the coolness from the earth that kept it cool all the time. We put potatoes down there. He had an apple orchard over there, and we put apples down there; put it in paper brown bags—granny sacks they called them. And we would store them in the cellar, and all during winter we ate from there. We didn't have to go to the store. You might go to the store…well you didn't have to go to the store for milk because he had the cow. We made the cottage cheese and made bread, and then they did the butter.*[78]

Post–World War II

As the war ended and Black veterans returned to Northern Virginia, they still faced the harsh reality of segregation and racism. Neighborhoods were still separated by color. Home associations installed covenants that prohibited Black people from buying homes in White neighborhoods. Blacks were barred from swimming pools and other local amusement parks such as Marshall Hall and Glen Echo. But the African Americans in Merrifield and the surrounding areas did not let racism stop them from enjoying life. They couldn't go to Ocean City, so instead they went to Carl's or Sparrows beach in Annapolis, Maryland. Coney Island in New York was a spot they frequented for amusement park thrills. To offset the lack of swimming pools available to Black children, the Northern Virginia Baptist Association, of which First Baptist of Merrifield is a member, built its own pool in 1960 to teach African American children to swim. Because Truman had desegregated the military, that also meant the swimming pools on post and bases were desegregated. Freddie, who worked at Fort Myer, knew many of the military personnel, and they would invite me to join their families at the swimming pool on the post. In later years, we were able to go to Lake Fairfax and swim, but the Black swimmers would have to wear swim caps because management feared that our hair would clog up the drains. Bull Run Regional Park is my first memory of a truly integrated swimming facility, where no one had to wear a bathing cap unless they wanted to wear one.

Voting was another issue with the veterans returning from the war. Freddie was required to pay a poll tax before he was allowed to vote. This type of voter intimidation was finally outlawed with the Voting Rights Act of 1965. I vividly remember how my mother would drive anyone who needed a ride to the polling booth to vote. She also would take me into the polling booth with her as she cast her ballot. She instilled in me the obligation of voting because so many Black lives were lost to obtain this right.

From Reconstruction to the mid-1960s, the Blacks in Merrifield, the Pines and Williamstown worked hard to create a society where there were safety nets to protect them from bigotry. They established a church, and it worked in tandem with the schools and the students in providing a better way of life. Most owned their own land and homes. They had government jobs or opened their own businesses. They knew where to travel and where not to travel. They built bridges over racist ideology to create an ideal existence for their families and neighbors. But by the end of the 1960s, the African American communities of the Pines and Merrifield no longer existed. Fairfax County was changing from a rural, sleepy part of Virginia that just happened to be several miles from the nation's capital into a juggernaut of business and neighborhoods—White neighborhoods. With its slowness in building an African American high school, dragging its feet to desegregate and using the means to acquire Black folks' land through eminent domain and sanitation requirements, the county was still showing its racism. These topics are explored in the Pines chapter of the book.

SEGREGATED ENTERTAINMENT AND FAMILY LIFE

The 1902 Virginia Constitutional Convention effectively disenfranchised Black individuals, leading to the widespread adoption of Jim Crow laws in Virginia. As a result, African American residents of Fairfax County faced numerous challenges imposed by segregation. Decades later, several residents of Merrifield participated in an oral history project for the Northern Virginia Civil Rights Archive. Velma Johnson Massenberg and William Smith, both African Americans, recounted their experiences and the realities of living under laws that enforced segregation and unequal treatment of people of color.

When discussing the issue of segregation, Velma noted that people were not inherently hostile. Instead, she emphasized that Black individuals were aware of which places were appropriate to visit and which to avoid. She also pointed out that while Merrifield and the Providence District are classified as part of the South, they are not considered part of the Deep South. As a result, people lived separately but peacefully. Velma shared that the only time she was called the N-word was when she and her girlfriend tried to rent an apartment at Pine Springs in Falls Church. With the passage of the Civil Rights Bill, Velma felt empowered to rent an apartment and live independently in an area that had been segregated. Unfortunately, when she went to apply, the leasing office was closed. As she was returning to her car, a White resident yelled, "We don't want any N-----s here."[79] As a caveat to this story, in 1982 I rented an apartment in Pine Springs, the very apartment complex that years earlier was not welcoming to Velma and Blacks.

Velma's family history is quite interesting. Her father, Mr. James Johnson, owned several businesses, including a landscaping company and a trash removal service. He was also a member and trustee of the First Baptist Church of Merrifield. Mr. Johnson was a visionary who understood the importance of generational wealth. In the 1950s, he leased his 3.5 acres of land to a developer who aimed to construct apartments for African Americans. These apartments, located on Hollywood Road, were named Hollywood Gardens.[80] This initiative to provide affordable housing for Black residents was revolutionary. On one side of Lee Highway were Hollywood Gardens for Black tenants, while on the other side stood Pine Springs Apartments for White residents. Since the developers of Hollywood Gardens only leased the land, Mr. Johnson had an apartment within the complex. In the early 2000s, Velma and her family sold the land. It was then purchased by another developer who built a community called Hopkins Glen. This area is located across from the National Cemetery on the corner of Lee Highway and Hollywood Drive.

Velma grew up attending the old Merrifield church, where she sang in the choir, and later in the new church, she organized a little children's and a youth choir. Velma remembers how when the Merrifield Drive-In Theater

Gospel Messenger Chorus anniversary celebration in the fellowship hall of First Baptist Church of Merrifield. Pictured from left to right are Ms. Ruth Johnson and Edith Collins-Terry. Directly behind Edith Terry is Trustee James Johnson. To Mr. Johnson's right is Ms. Taylor. She owned her own beauty shop in Merrifield. *Courtesy of Robert "Bobbi" Whitmore.*

was opened, it was segregated. She said Blacks couldn't go to that drive-in, but they had one in Manassas they attended. Old-timers may remember the Jefferson Theater and the State Theater in Falls Church. All these facilities were segregated. But to offset this racism, on occasion, the First Baptist Church would have a movie night.

When Velma entered the segregated school system in Fairfax County, she was nine years old. She attended James Lee Elementary School from the fourth to the seventh grade. In the eighth grade, she moved on to Luther Jackson High School on Gallows Road in Merrifield, where she completed her education. Velma was one of sixty-five graduates in her class at Luther Jackson High School. This would also be the last class to graduate from Luther Jackson High.

Velma talked about being a cheerleader for the All-Black football team. The high school also had a basketball team and offered various activities, including choir, music programs and home economics. The teachers, all of

Top: Raising the American flag at Luther Jackson, a segregated high school in Merrifield, Virginia. The school opened in 1954 for grades one through twelve and then changed to eight through twelve in 1957. *Courtesy of Fairfax County School Board History website.*

Bottom: Griffith Stadium in Washington, D.C., home of the Washington Senators baseball team. The stands were segregated, and African American attendees sat on the right side of the field. The date is unknown but is probably late '40s or early '50s. *Photo provided by author.*

whom were Black, treated the students like their own children, nurturing and supporting them while encouraging them to succeed. As a result, many graduates went on to become lawyers, engineers and professionals in academia.

Unfortunately, when schools were desegregated, Velma witnessed many Black students who felt unwelcome in the newly integrated school system. Students of color often felt marginalized and unrecognized. Velma mentioned that Black athletes from Luther Jackson, who integrated into White schools, were not allowed to join the football or basketball teams. Many students felt that the White teachers did not care for them as much as their African American instructors had. I can attest to this sentiment, as I experienced similar feelings at Oakton High School as recently as 1978.

One thing that was always emphasized to her was the importance of the "right to vote."[81] She recalled that her parents were registered voters who participated in every election, just as she does. Additionally, Velma had a memorable experience when President Barack Obama visited her home and had dinner with her family during his presidency.

Another interview was with William Smith, the grandson of Seth Williams, the founder of Williamstown. William grew up in Williamstown, near his grandfather. Seth spoke about growing up in Merrifield during segregation. As with Velma, William felt important at Luther Jackson High. He felt that the teachers cared. He also spoke of the segregated Merrifield Drive-In Theater and how his family also went to the drive-in in Manassas. When Fairfax Hospital opened in 1960, William noted that the hospital was not very nice to Black folks. Now Fairfax Hospital, or INOVA, is a world-class facility, especially dealing with the conditions of the heart. My aunt, Dovella McCormick, who grew up in the Pines, was an LPN, and she worked in the anesthesiology department of the hospital. She is also noted as being one of the first Black nurses hired at Arlington Hospital in Arlington, Virginia.

Outdoor events and travel were difficult for African Americans in Northern Virginia. If you were to take a drive in the country through Leesburg or Middleburg, there were no restaurants readily available to people of color. So, you would pack lunches of fried chicken and boiled eggs and eat on the side of the road. Even at professional sporting events, such as those involving the Washington Senators baseball team in Washington, D.C., African Americans were confined to the colored section, which was situated on the right side of the playing field. Eulala Lee Ransell loved baseball and often visited Griffith Stadium with her father, Avon.

CHAPTER 3

MERRIFIELD SCHOOLS

Southern enslavers' greatest fear was being murdered in their sleep or poisoned by the person they held in bondage. After Nat Turner, a free man of color, failed at an attempt to end slavery, southerners' fears grew more dramatic. In 1831, because Turner was a literate preacher, the South felt that his education was the ignition that lit the fuse of rebellion. However, even before Nat Turner's uprising of 1831, Virginia had already passed a law declaring that no enslaved person could learn or attend school. But by 1832, most southern states, including Virginia, had passed and imposed stronger laws to control literacy within both the enslaved and free African American populations. Virginia's law stated that any assembly to teach the enslaved or free persons to read or write was illegal.[82] As Frederick Douglass once said, "Once you learn to read you will be forever free."[83] Douglass knew that literacy was transformative and provided an avenue to power and true freedom, none of which the enslaved or free persons were given.

On January 1, 1863, implementation of the Emancipation Proclamation changed things. As Benjamin Brawley noted in *A Social History of the American Negro*, "At the close of the Civil War the United States found itself face to face with one of the gravest social problems of modern times. More and more it became apparent that it was not only the technical question of the restoration of the states to the Union that had to be considered, but the whole adjustment for the future of the lives of three and a half million Negroes…in the South."[84] Fairfax County had its own problems with what to do with the newly freed. Freedmen's Bureau records reported on January 1, 1863, that approximately 2,167 newly freed enslaved and 774 freed African Americans were living in Fairfax County.[85] However, only 128 could read, with 2,813 literate and 539 listed as unable to care for themselves, per the bureau's National Archives Microfilm Publication M1055, Roll 21, "Miscellaneous Reports and Lists," for 1865–69.[86]

After the Civil War, even with limited formal education, African Americans sought to obtain land, become educated and create their own religious institutions.[87] These three elements—landownership, religious autonomy and educational opportunities—were vital to their success during the Reconstruction era. Mills-Crossroads also fell into this pattern during this time. Freedmen such as Joshua Ball, Nimrod Dixon and Horace Gibson were the first Black land purchasers in Mills-Crossroads. Once Ball, Nimrod and Gibson, along with other Freedmen, acquired their homesteads, they created a community with a religious institution called the First Baptist Church of Merrifield and educational opportunities for their children. Documentation from the Reconstruction era substantiates the willingness of freemen, like those at Mills-Crossroads, to create their communities and churches. A census worker for the federal government, right after the Civil War, noted in an official report, "The Virginia Negroes were exceptionally progressive....[They] seem to look for an improvement in their condition more to their own exertions and to local action, and less to the general Government and the people of the North."[88] From 1864 until 1868, the Freedmen's Bureau of Fairfax County established and supported fifteen schools for African American students: Andrew's Chapel, Camp Wadsworth Upper Farm, Centreville, Falls Church, Gum Springs, Lewinsville, Painter's School, Woodlawn (Accotink), Big Falls (Great Falls), Camp Wadsworth Lower Farm, Fairfax County Court House, Frying Pan (Herndon), Langley, Lincoln Village and Vienna. There was no school for students in the Merrifield area at this time. Those who wished to attend school had to go to Falls Church Negro School.[89]

In June 1870, Virginia passed the Public Free School Act, which entitled children to a free education. Four years after the act, land was purchased from J.W. Gaylord and his wife to build an all-White educational institution in Mills-Crossroads. Unfortunately, it took another twenty-four years before the Fairfax County School Board designated an elementary school for educating children of color in that same area. However, the establishment of a White school in Mills-Crossroads was in progress, as the notes for the Merrifield White school indicate:

- *1874: Deed of Purchase: Fairfax Deed Book R-4:439, Oct. 8, 1874: Tobias Robey, Robert S. Porter, Charles Arnold, John Brenizer, and Jone Darne, trustees, purchase 43 poles of land from J.W. Gaylord and Mary, his wife, for use as a schoolhouse and for religious services. (Later records refer to this as Parcel 1 of the property of the Merrifield Improvement Association lot. The school system did not retain claim to this property, and it was not transferred in a blanket deed.)*[90]
- *1878: There is a white school in Merrifield (Mills-Crossroads) on the G.M. Hopkins Map, 1878–79.*
- *1884: Deed of Purchase: Fairfax Deed Book D-5:362, June 7, 1884: The School Trustees of Providence District purchase 43 poles of land from Robert Porter and Camilla, his wife. (They were purchasing additional land to enlarge the school lot).*[91]

The deed of purchase for the White schoolhouse land included strict stipulations that mandated the school building be exclusively utilized for White students. Failure to enforce this provision would result in the land reverting to the original owners, J.W. Gaylord and his wife, or their heirs. In 1898, the one-room Black schoolhouse was opened in Merrifield, Virginia.

By 1905, other areas of unequal treatment were seen in the teachers' monthly salaries. White male teachers earned $40.77 per month, and White female instructors were paid $33.36. In the same year, it is not surprising that the African American faculty members were paid far less. Black male instructors received $29.78 per month, and their female counterparts earned the lowest at $20.29 per month.

The majority of First Baptist Church of Merrifield's written records are lost, but oral history tells us that the church was used as a place of education well before the first wooden beam was placed for the Black schoolhouse in 1898. History tells us that the use of a religious facility as a school was not uncommon in the Black community. Sabbath and normal schools were noted as being held in homes and African American churches until land was acquired and a proper schoolhouse was erected. One example is Second Baptist Church in Falls Church, Virginia, established in 1872. The sanctuary was used as a public school during the week and a religious institution on Sundays. Prior to the construction of the Mills-Crossroads school, it is assumed that some Black students first attended the Falls Church Colored School.

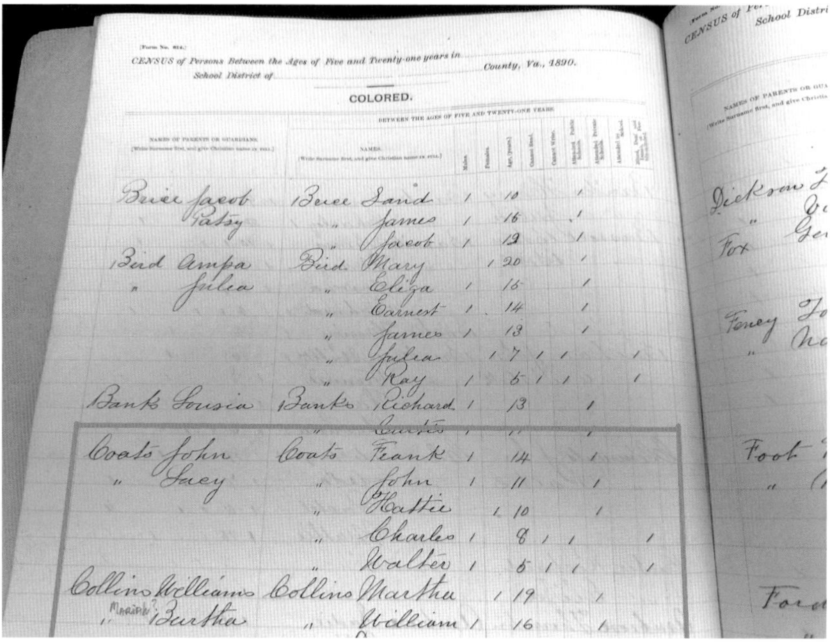
[Form No. 814.]
CENSUS of Persons Between the Ages of Five and Twenty-one years in ______ County, Va., 1890.
School District of ______

COLORED.

Names of Parents or Guardians	Names	Males	Females	Age
Brice Jacob	Brice Sand	1		10
Patsy	" James	1		16
	" Jacob	1		19
Bird Ampa	Bird Mary		1	20
" Julia	" Eliza	1		15
	" Earnest	1		14
	" James	1		13
	" Julia		1	7
	" Ray	1		5
Bank Lousia	Banks Richard	1		13
	" Curtis	1		11
Coats John	Coats Frank	1		14
" Lucy	" John	1		11
	" Hattie		1	10
	" Charles	1		8
	" Walter	1		5
Collins Williams	Collins Martha		1	19
" Mariah? Bertha	" William	1		16

The 1890 school census for the "Colored School" in Falls Church Virginia. John E. Coats and William Collins Sr., both from Mills-Crossroads, enrolled their children into the school for the 1890 school session. Under William Collins is his wife, Mariah Bertha Collins. *Photo provided by the Fairfax County Archives.*

The *Falls Church Pulse* reported that a school for African American students had started:

> *One bright spot occurred in 1888 when the Society of Friends (Quakers) built the Falls Church Colored School with support from the Providence District of Fairfax County. Land was donated by James Lee, and a two-room schoolhouse was erected. The school was just a building without running water and with outhouses for toilets and a pot belly stove in the middle of the building that provided the classes heat in winter.*[92]

It can be assumed that Mills-Crossroads sent its students to the Falls Church school until its school was constructed. Ms. A.S. Gray was reported as the instructor, and her monthly salary was twenty-five dollars.

The Merrifield school enrolled students of color from first grade to the seventh grade, but there was no eighth-grade or higher-level classes for Black people in the county until Manassas Regional High School was created.

Residents in the Mills-Crossroads and Gravel Bank area registered their children per the 1890 "Census of School Population."[93] John Coates in 1890 enrolled his children—Hattie, Charlie, Walter, Essie, Ulis and Everett Coates—into school. William Collins Sr. followed suit by registering his daughter, Martha, and two sons, William Jr. and Douglas Collins. Richard Robinson was listed as the parent or guardian for the registration of Will, Agnes, Jerry, Charles, Grace and Richard. Another parent was Richard Slaughter, who enrolled Eva, Richard, Milton, Rosa and Destimona. Interestingly, Martha Collins's age was listed as nineteen when she registered for this school term. The schoolhouse for Mills-Crossroads Black students wasn't opened until 1898, therefore they were sending their children to the Falls Church Colored School, or the church was providing the educational services.[94]

The "colored" school on Porter Road, when built, lacked basic facilities like running water, bathrooms and central heating, except for a large potbellied stove. This was the school attended by my grandmother Myra and later her daughters. The children from the neighboring Pines community had to walk two miles one way to get to this school. But other Black students, like Viola Johnson from Ilda, near Little River Turnpike, had to endure a three-mile hike.[95] These conditions highlight the challenges and disparities faced by Black students, emphasizing the urgent need for improved educational facilities. Yet the Fairfax County School Board turned a blind eye to the needs of its African American students.

When Avonjeanette was of age to attend school, she was enrolled into the Merrifield Colored School. She attended classes from grades one to three, and then for fourth grade, she transferred to a new two-room wooden schoolhouse down the street. The larger school was built in 1939 and was located behind what is now McDonald's on Gallows Road. However, when my mother was in school, there was no upper-level education available for Black students in Fairfax. Both my mother and grandmother were limited to a seventh-grade education.

Helen Haight of the Pines shared a story about how during winter, the teacher would prepare a basin of hot water for the students as they arrived at school.[96] The students' fingers were often cold and frozen, so the teacher would have them soak their hands in the warm water to get their blood flowing. Since there was no running water, the teacher had to pump water from the well outside and then heat it on the potbellied stove. Additionally, because there were no janitorial services, both the teacher and the students were responsible for keeping the school clean.

This included the male students having to chop the wood needed to keep the stove running and the building warm during winter. Annual surveys of the school's physical property reported that the Merrifield school lacked maps, and that the teacher's desk was broken. The White schools were given up-to-date amenities.

Even with inequality, the First Baptist Church of Merrifield and the Colored School on Porter Road worked in tandem to ensure that the Black students of the community would have an education, even though the students were given hand-me-down schoolbooks from the White students and dilapidated school supplies. The teachers and parents made the best of an unequal situation. The interesting part is that students in Merrifield attended the same church and the same school, which made for a close-knit community.

Teachers at the Black schools were just like their White counterparts. Although the one-room schoolhouse was small for gatherings of both students and parents, they held programs at the church, where larger crowds could be accommodated. Black instructors also ensured that the students were aware of the heroes of their race, including Frederick Douglass, Harriet Tubman and Booker T. Washington, among others. Conversely, school board notes taken in November 1922 clearly show the concern for the White Merrifield School and supplies purchased. However, there is no mention of the "colored" school and supplies needed or procured:

- *1922, Nov. 13: Meeting #8: Supplies were purchased for Wakefield, Burke, Belle Aire and Oak Grove (white). Blackboards were purchased for Woodlawn and Springfield. Bills were paid for Oakton, Chesterbrook, Merrifield (white), Idylwood, Andrew Chapel, and McLean (Franklin Sherman).*
- *1924, Aug. 19: Meeting #4: The Board resolved that a school building of at least three rooms should be provided at Merrifield (white school) within a year and that an application for a loan from the Literary Fund for this purpose be sent in as soon as plans and specifications could be prepared.*

On February 22, 1935, another all-White high school opened its doors for the students of Fairfax. It was all brick with indoor plumbing and heating. Two years later, in October 1938, the school board agreed to build a White elementary school at Dunn Loring. "The building would consist of five classrooms and an auditorium large enough to seat 250 people. Mr. A.C.

Photo of first Merrifield "Colored School," built in 1898. The photo was taken in the 1940s for insurance purposes. *Courtesy of Avonjeannette Hill.*

Photo of a play at the original First Baptist Church of Merrifield titled *Heaven's Gate*. The girl on the right-hand side, in front of the lady in a hat, is the author. *Courtesy of Robert "Bobbi" Whitmore.*

Martin, an employee of the Federal government, as well as a community-minded citizen, presented a plan for building the school and spearheaded activities to raise the funds necessary for its construction."[97]

For years, Mary Ellen Henderson, affectionately known as "Miss Nelly," and other African American parents pushed for better accommodation for their children. Their actions resulted in the opening of James Lee Elementary for Black students in 1948. In an oral history interview, Mr. Paul Jones Jr. proudly recalled the elementary school's modern amenities with an all-brick building, good floors and indoor plumbing. He said that they no longer had to clean the floors with linseed oil, which was a fire hazard given the use of the stove for heat. He vividly described transitioning from a one-room schoolhouse in Merrifield to a two-room school before his father transferred him to Falls Church Elementary. This action to move Paul to Falls Church was taken after his brother was unfairly dismissed from Merrifield school due to a disability. Mr. Jones reflected that in those days, there were no special education classes.[98]

The differences between the Merrifield Colored School and the New James Lee Elementary were striking. Paul remembered vividly that the children at the James Lee school took castor oil to keep them well. Dr. Johnson, the only Black physician in Falls Church, would come and give them free physicals. Also, Dr. Ellison, a Black dentist, came and gave them free dental exams.[99] Paul continued his education at the newly opened James Lee Elementary and remained dedicated to his studies.[100] James Lee Elementary remained segregated until 1966, even though Fairfax County was ordered to start desegregating in 1954 after *Brown v. Board of Education*. The elementary school was then repurposed after desegregation and is now the James Lee Community Center.

Returning to the 1938 school year, the Fairfax County School Board convened to discuss the budget for the year. One of the topics under consideration was the construction of a new school for Black students in Merrifield. According to the *Washington Post*, the Fairfax County School Board announced plans for the construction of new schools. Superintendent W.T. Woodson, who was White and known to support segregation, revealed plans for a new high school in Mount Vernon and a new brick elementary school in Dunn Loring for White children. The board agreed to establish a two-room wooden elementary school for African American students in Merrifield, but there was no mention of building a high school.[101]

The lack of action afforded to the African American students highlighted the clear inequality within the school system. It is undeniable that the building cost for the White elementary school far exceeded the wood-framed "colored" school—the cost of the White school was budgeted at $50,000, and the Merrifield school simply cost $3,450. These prices are in addition to the expansion of the all-White Fairfax High School and several other schools in Springfield and Annandale. However, by 1938, there was still no higher levels of learning past the seventh grade for African American students in Fairfax.[102]

When the construction of both buildings was completed, a comparison of the schools was striking. Dunn Loring Elementary School was a sturdy brick building with an auditorium that seated 250 people. The White school had five classrooms, central heating and janitorial staff. The students had indoor plumbing and bathrooms. In contrast, the Black school was a small, two-room framed building that still relied on a potbellied stove for warmth. The faculty and students cleaned the building, and there was no indoor plumbing, so they still had to rely on an outhouse.

With transition in the air, on January 6, 1939, Avonjeanette Lee embarked on a new chapter as she entered the newly built wooden schoolhouse in Merrifield for African American students. Finally, the Fairfax School Board was addressing the issue of overcrowding of the one-room school founded in 1898. Prior to constructing the second school, the overcrowding had gotten so bad that the Odd Fellows Hall, on Gallows Road, had to be used as an overflow educational facility for many Black students. Many younger adults, unable to continue their education past the seventh grade, chose to take night classes or training courses at the Merrifield Odd Fellows Hall. My mother took several courses, one in hair dressing and another in photography. Many of the pictures in this book were taken by my mother with her Brownie camera. Although Dunn Loring Elementary was right down the road, under Jim Crow, classrooms were legally segregated.

The 1939 school year was good for Avonjeanette, as she found solace in the faculty at the new school. One teacher made a lasting impression on her. This instructor was a gymnastics enthusiast and taught the children "hoop drills."[103] Avonjeanette explained that the students would decorate their hoops and jump through them. Their precision and skill led to invitations to display their abilities at other schools.[104] Also, the plays and pageants continued, but with an additional classroom, the performances were held at the school rather than at the church. However, due to increased student population, the original one-room schoolhouse on Porter Road was still needed for instruction for some African American students.

It must be stated again that people of color had no brick-and-mortar high school within Fairfax County until Luther Jackson High opened in 1954—

The second, wooden "colored" schoolhouse, built in 1939, located behind what is now the McDonald's on Gallows Road and near Mr. George Hyson's home. *Courtesy of the Fairfax County School Board.*

the same year *Brown v. Board of Education* required schools to desegregate. However, many students did not let the lack of schooling in Fairfax stop them from obtaining a higher education. Many paid tuition to attend "Dunbar, Cardoza, or Armstrong High Schools or Phelps Vocation Center in Washington, D.C."[105]

CHAPTER 4

FAIRFAX COUNTY COLORED CITIZENS ASSOCIATION

Starting in September 1928, African Americans in the county organized the Fairfax County Colored Citizens Association. Its first president was Harrison R. Tinner, a resident of Merrifield, and the second president was Rufus Hamilton. The purpose of the organization was to "organize the Negroes in Fairfax County, VA for the purpose of voting in all elections." The organization aimed to "[b]etter Negro citizenship in Fairfax County through its stand for: a fuller use of the ballot by all Negroes, greater improvement in Colored schools, Justice in the courts and public convenances [*sic*], Active participation in all county and civic affairs, Promotion of a better feeling between the races and to booster the county as a desirable place to live"[106] In its thirty-year anniversary brochure, the organization listed the founders as Harrison Tinner, C.V. Hyson and Joseph Collins of Merrifield; A.G. Murray and Ollie W. Turner of Falls Church; and R.J. Evans, William Ball, Lula Robinson, Margaret Tinner, A.E. Simonson, Melvin Tinner, Martha Wade, John Jones, Maggie Brown and Walter Hyson.

There were many accomplishments within the thirty years since its founding. In 1937, it aided in passing a more equitable bond that provided better treatment in Black education.[107] It spearheaded writing letters to Congress in support of the anti-lynching bill. The organization increased voter registration within Fairfax from 57 voters in 1928 to 782 in 1941.[108] It created voters clubs in Gums Springs, Woodlawn and Falls Church. Within the realm of education, the organization demanded the state board of education provide the same share of funds for Black schools as White. It also required construction of toilet facilities within Black elementary schools, as this was state law.[109] In May 1935, men from this organization including Alexander L. White, Otis Wade, Atanar Payne, John R. Pearson, Joseph Collins of Merrifield, Henry Page and Ollie W. Tinner were the first Blacks to be seated on a jury in Fairfax County.[110] Other affiliated organizations included the National Association for the Advancement of Colored People (NAACP), Federation of Colored School Leagues, Negro Organization Society of Virginia and the Fairfax County Tuberculosis Association. In the decade following the 1940s, the community heard from prominent individuals such as Reverend Costner of Fall Church and Reverend Sheppard, advocating for a high school in Fairfax County for Black students. These men were activists as well as prominent members and leaders within the Fairfax County Colored Citizens Association. This association was a driving force for advocating and finally achieving a Black high school within the borders of the county. But before this happened, there was Manassas Regional High School for Black students.

Chapter 5

MANASSAS REGIONAL HIGH SCHOOL

The solution to the lack of a Black high school for students in Fairfax was simple to the all-White schoolboard. Within the boundaries of Prince William County, Virginia, there was a vocational institute called the Manassas Industrial School for Colored Youth. Organized in 1894, it was the dream child of a former slave named Jennie Dean. Her goal was to provide a quality, vocational education for Black students. With pressure from local Black leaders to provide classes past the seventh grade, in the fall of 1937–38 school year Fairfax County paid for its African American students to attend what was now the Manassas High School. In June 1938, Fairfax County, along with Fauquier and Prince William Counties, purchased Jennie Dean's old school and created the Manassas Regional High School.[111]

The founder, Mrs. Dean, had been enslaved in Prince William County near Pageland Road, which sits next to the modern-day Manassas Battlefield National Park. There she lived with her mother, father, siblings and grandparents. She was alive when the First and Second Battles of Manassas took place, and as the cannons became silent, her father worked to bury both the Union and Confederate soldiers killed in the conflict.

After the war, Jennie felt a strong desire to help "her people" in schooling. She started churches and her own Sabbath schools and taught vocational skills to her neighbors and friends. Jennie knew that this would not be enough for Blacks to get ahead. They needed higher levels of education and vocational training. So, Jennie took it upon herself to start the Manassas Industrial School for Colored Youth. With a campus of more than one

Leola Lee Pearson's graduation photo from the Manassas Regional High School. *Courtesy of author.*

hundred acres, the school opened its doors in September 1894, with the honorable and widely respected Frederick Douglass giving the opening address at the dedication. Clara Barton, the founder of the Red Cross, was also at the dedication ceremony. Noteworthy White people such as Emily Howland and Andrew Carnegie supported the school in many ways. Jennie's vision of a place of higher learning lasted until 1938, when it was purchased and turned into a regional high school for the surrounding jurisdiction. It is estimated that more than six thousand young Black adults walked the halls of both the industrial and the regional high schools.

After completing the seventh grade in Merrifield, Avonjeanette and her four sisters—Irene, Dovella, Hazel and Leola Lee—all had an opportunity to attend the Manassas Regional High School. Dovella, after obtaining her academic diploma, went on to become an LPN and was one of the first Black nurses hired at Arlington Hospital in Arlington, Virginia. Leola was a valedictorian of her class. She was also an accomplished pianist. Avonjeannete was named homecoming queen at Manassas and played piano on various talent shows aired on the local radio stations in Washington, D.C.

The following was written on September 2, 1937, in the Fairfax County School minutes:

> *The Division Superintendent reported that he had met with representatives of the Fairfax County Colored Citizens Association with reference to bus transportation of high school children in Fairfax County to the regional Negro high school at Manassas. He reported that it appeared that two buses would be necessary to touch points indicated below with the approximate number of children indicated opposite each to be picked up at these points. Route No. 1: Woodlawn—8; Gum Spring- 10; Spring Bank—12; Baileys—9; Mt. Pleasant—8; to Manassas, estimated distance 42 miles. Route No. 2: Sideburn—4; Merrifield—5; Falls Church—5; Tysons—*[blank]*; Vienna—7; Fairfax—11; Chantilly—2; to Manassas, estimated mileage 43.*[112]

The plan to bus Black students to Manassas Regional High School from as far away as Route 1, Woodlawn and Gum Springs seems absurd to modern thinking. The students were forced to ride one of two buses for upward of two hours to reach their designated high school.

It would be an understatement to say that all was not rosy for Fairfax students attending the Manassas School. Avonjeanette and her sisters would walk the two miles to Merrifield to catch the school bus. When boarding the bus, the cold frost of winter would hit their body, as the bus was old, had no heat and broke down frequently. The transportation to the school was always crowded. The bus had bench seats that faced each other and was often driven by fellow students at the school. In the fall and early spring, if it was hot, the students would roll down the windows for air circulation. With the windows down and many of the streets unpaved and rustic, the dust from the road would cover their clothes even before they came to class. During the school's existence, students from the school were hired as bus drivers. They would pick up their fellow classmates, take them to school, go to their classes and then, at the end of the day, drive the students home.

Helen Haight says that when she went to Manassas, the heat did not work in the winter, and you had to wear your coat all day around campus.[113] Most astonishing was how Avonjeanette pointed out that she was unable to register for the classes necessary to graduate. As the school was in Prince William County, those students had priority in selecting their courses. Subsequently, when Fairfax students attempted to register for classes, they often found that they were already full.[114]

The conditions of this school fell short of the "separate but equal" philosophy of Jim Crow America. Ironically, for the Lee daughters and their cousin Helen Haight, they were bused past several White schools, such as Fairfax High. Other areas needing attention included the overcrowded classrooms, which forced many spaces, such as the auditorium or cafeteria, to be used to facilitate learning classrooms.

Chapter 6

LUTHER JACKSON HIGH SCHOOL

Named after Luther Jackson, an African American historian who earned a PhD and spent his life researching, writing and educating Black citizens on their history, Luther Jackson High School became the only African American high school in Fairfax. Jackson was a strong advocate for equality in education, and it seemed appropriate to name the school after him. When land was purchased for the high school, though, it was initially called the Merrifield Colored School. Land records from Fairfax County Deed Book 910, show that on September 7, 1951, 14.415 acres of land were purchased from Ottomarius Enid Stone Faison. In January 1952, an additional 6,616 acres of land were purchased from Consuelo A. Seoane and Corita G. Seoane, according to Fairfax County Deed Book 942. The land acquisition from Faison was orchestrated with the help of Ollie Tinner, an African American leader in Falls Church, Virginia.

When Luther Jackson was officially built, named and dedicated, it was a school that also housed elementary students from the African American community. From 1954 to 1956, elementary students were taught within the walls of Luther Jackson. In 1957, the school no longer had elementary students, but it did have grades eight through twelve.

For the next eleven years, from 1954 to 1965, Luther Jackson was segregated. Many of my cousins, such as Guy Jr. and Rose Marie Collins, graduated from this school. Rose and Guy were Guy Collins Sr.'s children. Guy Sr. was listed as the official piano technician for Luther Jackson, and his wife, Edna Payne Collins, was the secretary of the PTA. My Aunt Myra

Photo of elementary classroom at Luther Jackson High school, March 17, 1955. Ernestine Moss-Baker is in the sixth row in the next to last. *Courtesy of Ernestine Moss-Baker.*

Richards was a crossing guard. These students and their families cherished this institution. Black folks felt a sense of pride, as they now had their own higher-level education facility. Most importantly, the students at Luther Jackson were not going to be denied a formal academic diploma like some of their parents had been.

As the segregation laws dictated, Luther Jackson had its own Black football and basketball teams. Girls were on the drill team and cheerleading squads. Music was important to the overall academics, and there was choir and band instruction—all extracurricular. Other pupils trained in areas such as home economics and furniture repair. Leonard Lee, a student at the school, recalled that during the summer breaks, a local White businessman–owned furniture store called Lee Furniture would provide apprenticeships to students who wanted to learn furniture making and repairs. Lee Furniture was also a sponsor of the yearbook, called the *Tiger*.

I entered the school system in kindergarten in 1964–65, as Fairfax was attempting to desegregate. I was to attend Fairhill Elementary, but due to the uncertainty of desegregation, my mother placed me in a private kindergarten and first grade. I joined the White Holy Trinity Lutheran Church School in

Luther Jackson High School band and majorettes. *Courtesy of Fairfax County Public School website.*

Falls Church. Pastor Niece was the principal, and there was not a nicer man to lead a congregation. In the summer of 1965–66, my four cousins and I would attend Holy Trinity's Vacation Bible School. One day, all the kids were outside lining up teams for kickball. One of the White students yelled out, "I don't want the niggers on my team!" When Pastor Niece was told of those comments, he immediately addressed it in a full assembly. He said to all the children that there was no room for this type of behavior in his church. He really was a White man ahead of his time.

In retrospect, it has not been easy for many Northern Virginia African American students starting from the Public-School Act of the 1870s through to the present. In the 1960s, Fairfax County closed the original Merrifield Colored School and auctioned it off. The one-room structure now had a new owner, who turned it into rental property. The building that showcased the county's disregard for the educational needs of Black students was still standing when I was a child. I grew up across the street from the school, but by then it had been converted into a one-room home, still without running water and indoor plumbing. I used to play with a girl who lived in the old schoolhouse that turned into a residential home. The irony is that I visited the space where my grandmother, mother and aunts once were taught in an unequal, segregated school system.

By 1966, even after 1954's *Brown v. Board of Education* Supreme Court decision to strike down segregation, the county had still not fully integrated its schools. Following are newspaper articles, both local and national starting in 1953, that provide a timeline of understanding the difficulties African

American communities had with the process of integration of the county's public school system.

According to the *Chicago Defender* article "Hint Plots to Balk School Integration" from April 18, 1953, the Fairfax County School Board probably would have canceled its agreement with Fort Belvoir and withdrawn its teachers from there if segregation in the post schools were ended in line with White House policy to end segregation in all schools operated on army posts with federal funds. Robert Walker, a Fairfax school official, noted that the county school board would have no other choice if school segregation were abolished at Fort Belvoir.[115]

From the *Washington Post*'s May 21, 1954, article "Still 'Part of Virginia'—Fairfax Continues Plans for Separate Schools," the Fairfax County School Board was going ahead with plans for separate housing of White and African American students for the 1954–55 school year despite the U.S. Supreme Court's decision banning school segregation. "We are still a part of the state of Virginia," declared Superintendent of Schools W. T. Woodson, "and cannot act as a separate subdivision like the District of Columbia. We'll plan for next year on the same basis as we have in the past." School Board member Fred Robinson said, "We're working just as we always have—there will be no change until we hear from the State Department of Education."[116]

In the *Washington Post*'s August 21, 1959, article "26 Fairfax Negroes Ask U.S. Court to End School Segregation at Once," the NAACP attorneys for the plaintiffs in the lawsuit against the school board asked the court to place the burden of justifying any desegregation delay on FCPS officials.

In the *Washington Post*'s January 11, 1959, article "Fairfax Unit Pushes Plan on Schools," the Fairfax County School Board was under increasing pressure to take some sort of action on school desegregation. The Federation of Citizens Associations was circulating a draft resolution calling for the adoption of a program of gradual school desegregation.

Under School Superintendent W.T. Woodson, a desegregation plan was created to integrate the schools through a "Grade a Year Policy." This process would take approximately twelve years for the county to fully desegregate its school system. In addition to the delays, Black students had to fill out an intent application to be transferred to White schools. Many of these students' applications to attend White schools closer to their homes were denied.

According to the *Washington Evening/Sunday Star*'s September 9, 1960, article "Fairfax Negroes Fight Grade-a-Year Policy," federal judge Albert V. Bryan of Alexandria adjourned a hearing for twenty-six Fairfax County Black children whose applications to enter White schools were rejected.

James M. Nabrit III, attorney for the children, told Judge Bryan during a seven-hour hearing that the school board's grade-per-year desegregation plan amounted to a delay. He attacked criteria under which the board had denied the applications. In July, the board told the court that it had devised a plan under which it would integrate only first and second grades during the 1960–61 school year and then integrate one grade each year thereafter. School Superintendent W.T. Woodson conceded that desegregation could move faster but said that this would produce "greater friction, and the learning capabilities of the children would be handicapped."

According to the *Washington Evening/Sunday Star*'s January 25, 1961, article "PTA Council Sustains Bi-Racial Sports Ban Student Protest," under consideration was the school board policy, set by a recent four-to-three vote, prohibiting integrated schools from fielding teams with White and Black members. Since the board's action, several hundred high school students have signed petitions protesting the decision. Two high schools were among the nine integrated county schools. One Black boy attended Groveton High School, Rayfield Barber, and a Black boy and girl attended James Madison. The resolution asking for the school board's reconsideration of the policy was offered by the Hollin Hills Elementary School PTA.[117]

According to the *Washington Evening/Sunday Star*'s June 28, 1963, article "Fairfax Changes Policy, Grants Negro Transfers," the Fairfax County School Board reversed a decision of the previous May and planned to admit five Black students to integrated schools farther from their homes than the all-Black schools to which they had been assigned. Fairfax County School Board members voted for the switch at a secret meeting the same day they learned that a Black attorney had filed suit seeking to force complete integration of the county's schools.

The *Washington Evening/Sunday Star*'s November 12, 1964, article "Fairfax Discontinuing All-Negro High School," plans were announced to eliminate Luther Jackson High School as an all-Black facility and turn it into an integrated intermediate school next September at the Fairfax County School Board meeting.

According to the *Washington Evening/Sunday Star*'s January 29, 1965, article "Fairfax Plan Would Complete County's School Integration," the last vestiges of a racially segregated school system in Fairfax County were to be wiped out over the next two years under a plan proposed by the Fairfax County School Board. Although Fairfax had been moving gradually toward full integration for several years, the new proposal was aimed at complying with a federal court order the previous summer that the "dual school system" end. Two of the county's five all-Black elementary schools, Lillian Carey and Drew-Smith, would become special education centers for children with disabilities and special needs soon. A third, Louise Archer, would become an integrated elementary facility next year. One of the remaining Black schools, Eleven Oaks, would be merged with a nearby predominantly White facility in September 1966. James Lee would be phased out, and the building would be used for an undetermined purpose.

According to the *Washington Post*'s November 17, 1966, article "Area Still Has Some Segregated Schools," the fall 1966 Fairfax County school enrollment stood at 3,520 Black and 98,312 White. "In Fairfax County, the degree of integration in individual schools varies from none to a Negro-white ratio of about 1-to-3 in Fairview and Louise Archer elementary schools. In only one school in Fairfax do Negroes outnumber white students: Parklawn, which is attended by 641 Negroes and 84 whites. Fairfax County integrated its last two Negro schools this fall."

With desegregation underway, Luther Jackson Negro High School was closed in 1964 and repurposed as an intermediate school for seventh and eighth graders. The James Lee Elementary School that Ms. Henderson and parents of color worked so hard to open was closed to student education. For years, it was repurposed as the Fairfax County Public School administrative offices. It is now a community center. Prior to desegregation, James Lee Elementary would have been my assigned school.

The desegregation process was long and challenging for many African Americans, and the experience at Luther Jackson changed significantly. While the segregated high school with an all-Black faculty had prioritized student success, the intermediate school and subsequent integrated high schools lacked attention for African American students and had an undercurrent of second-class citizenship. This is the type of environment I was in at Oakton High School in the 1970s. But as my neighbor Bobbi Whitmore, who is also Black and attended Oakton High School, stated, Black students were never treated fairly within the desegregated school system. For many, those years of desegregation from kindergarten through high school graduation were tumultuous. Some schools had police in the halls, and there was an air of uncertainty and a sense of dismissiveness by the White teachers and administrators. Because of isolation and disillusionment, my ability to have enough self-guided determination to go to college decades after I graduated from High School was enormous. I finally completed my undergraduate degree in 2012 from the University of Virginia (even though my high school counselor thought I wasn't smart enough). I then completed my Master of

Arts degree from George Mason University, and as of 2024, I am enrolled in the PhD program with a concentration of U.S. history.

Things are different now. There are no more one- or two-room schoolhouses that lack indoor plumbing, no more bus commutes lasting for two hours to get to classes and no more freezing classrooms. Now, the present-day Fairfax County School System boasts a diverse population of students. Fairfax County Public Schools (FCPS) has 199 schools, with a total enrollment of 1,185,980 pupils.[118] The average number of credits earned by each graduate is 29.4. The average division-wide high school ratio is 25.3 students for each teacher. The 2023–24 average per-pupil cost was $19,795. The 2022–23 school body in Fairfax County saw 36.9 percent White, 9.9 percent Black, 19.3 percent Asian/Pacific Islander, 27.4 percent Hispanic/Latino, 0.3 percent American Indian or Alaska Native and 0.1 percent Native Hawaiian or Pacific Islander.[119]

Per the *News and World Report*, the school system is now considered one of the best in the nation. Out of seventeen thousand schools, Thomas Jefferson High School for Science and Technology (TJHSST) in Fairfax County was named the top high school in Virginia and the United States for the fourth consecutive year, and several other FCPS high schools were ranked among the nation's best, including Langley High School at no. 136, McLean High School at no. 157, Marshall High School at no. 247 and my school, Oakton High, at no. 282. Most of these schools are in wealthy districts, where they have a low population of minority students.

Chapter 7

THE FIRST BAPTIST CHURCH OF MERRIFIELD

To appreciate the history of First Baptist Church of Merrifield, we must first look through a nineteenth-century lens into the historical context in which the church was established. In his book *Under Their Own Vine and Fig Tree: The African American Church in the South, 1865–1900*, William E. Montgomery maintained, "Blacks were striving to redefine their place in the economy. Their primary objective was the self-reliance their masters had denied them during slavery."[120] These denials encompassed education, religious autonomy, property ownership and control over their labor. To achieve true independence, many Freedmen left established White-owned homesteads in Fauquier County, as well as Alexandria's contraband camps, Roosevelt Island and Langley. They journeyed to areas where they could work, buy land and build their communities. One example is Alfred Odrick. Enslaved until emancipation, Alfred purchased twenty acres of land in McLean in 1872. Odrick's corner still exists to this day, and many of Odrick's descendants still live in the area. Once established, African American communities organized church congregations, such as First Baptist Vienna, Shiloh Baptist in McLean, Second Baptist of Falls Church, Chesterbrook and Galloway Methodist Church. Later, some of these families or their relatives moved to Mills-Crossroads and formed the First Baptist Church of Merrifield.

Furthermore, after the Civil War, some Black churches in Northern Virginia were created through the assistance of the Freedmen's Bureau,

A 1960s photo of First Baptist Church of Merrifield, facing Porter Road. *Courtesy of Avonjeannette Lee-Hill.*

northern benevolent groups such as the "Friends" or Quakers, White religious organizers, northern transplants and the Freedmen themselves. Blacks were determined to establish separate religious institutions led not by Whites but by "bone of their bone and flesh of their flesh."[121] The Black Christian institutions provided duality in both religious and normal school teachings. It also afforded African American men leadership roles in galvanizing their communities against the encroachment of inequality and the beginnings of Jim Crow.

In 2007, Avonjeanette Lee-Hill, a dedicated parishioner and descendant of an original member of the First Baptist Church of Merrifield, gave an oral history of the church's foundation. She noted that while the physical church building was established later, the organizational efforts to form a congregation started in the 1870s. In the absence of a building, parishioners would worship outside or, sometimes, at Second Baptist Church and later in a log cabin near Graham Road in Falls Church.[122] In Mills-Crossroads, historical documents reflect that Joshua Ball, Horace Gibson and Nimrod Nixon in the 1870s had the foresight for landownership, and some of these men would become instrumental in obtaining a permanent site of the First Baptist Church of Merrifield.

Flipping Land to Build a Church

After the war, in 1868, two White men, Robert Porter of Falls Church, Virginia, and his brother-in-law, J.W. Gaylord, living in New York, purchased through deferred payments 313 acres of land in trust at Mills-Crossroads from Andrew Gruman.[123] The 1868 deed registered December 10, 1868, reflects Andrew Gruman as the trustee of the property for John Glassell and his daughter Mildred S. Covall of Madison (Fauquier County), Virginia.[124] John Glassell obtained rights to the land through his marriage and marital contract to Margaret Scott-Lee in 1821.[125] Margaret married Glassell after the death of her second husband, Charles Lee. Charles was from the famous Lee family of Virginia, and he also served as U.S. secretary of state. His brother was Henry "Light-Horse Harry" Lee, notably the ninth governor of Virginia, who also fathered Robert E. Lee. To put things into perspective, the Providence District property was part of a larger tract of land owned by Charles and was divided among his heirs upon his death in 1815. When Margaret Lee married John Glassell in 1821, the marriage contract listed the 403 acres shown on the map provided by the Fairfax County History Commission.[126] Although they have Margaret as "Mary," other historical documents have her name as "Margaret." By the time of the Civil War, both Margaret and John were deceased, and in 1868, the land was in trust to Andrew Gruman. By 1874, Porter and Gaylord had obtained a clear deed to the property. Subsequently, this clear land deed allowed Robert Porter to begin selling parcels of land on the east side of Gallows Road to African Americans. However, the practice of selling to Blacks was not agreeable to some Whites in the Mills-Crossroads community.

Even with the wrath from the White citizens selling land tracts to Blacks, Robert Porter sold the land anyway, and in 1884, Porter sold five acres of property to Robert Bradley, an African American who later became quite successful.[127] In 1892, historical land deeds show that Bradley resold a parcel of land for one dollar to establish a Black Baptist church in Merrifield. Joshua Ball, Joshua Pearson and John Coates were formally listed as trustees on the deed.[128] However, in 1894, these three men in addition to Nimrod Dixon and William Stewart appeared as trustees for a new deed. An issue had surfaced with the first deed. When Bradley purchased the land from Porter, he didn't have a clear title when he sold the property for the purpose of building a church. The new deed in 1894 reflected a new purchase price of five dollars.[129]

Despite not being listed as trustees on the deed, other Black individuals played important roles in constructing the church building. William Collins Jr.

Photo of Jennie Collins-Ransell in the Pines. *Courtesy of author.*

and Mr. Phillip Luckett were instrumental in obtaining supplies for the construction, according to William's granddaughter Avonjeanette. "The 'Old Church' building began its humble beginnings with lumber purchased from the docks in nearby Alexandria, Virginia. William H. Collins Jr. and Mr. Phillip Luckett transported the building materials by horse and wagon to erect the original wooden edifice. A foundational platform was started and used as benches during worship services."[130] Avonjeanette also remembered stories of a young Jennie Ransell, who became the first pianist and later the mother of the church. "Jennie Ransell, a young child during this period, spoke of having her feet dangle between the beams of the floor, as she was young, and her legs were short."[131]

After they raised funds for siding, rafters and a roof, a devastating storm demolished the wooden structure, rendering it unusable. Undeterred, the faithful followers of Christ set out to rebuild. Despite taking many more years after the storm to finish the reconstruction, a new wooden structure was raised, and the cornerstone was laid in 1894. For African Americans in Merrifield, this landmark achievement was pivotal in establishing a community enriched with their deeply held values and morals. The freedom to worship, in stark contrast to being under an enslaver's control of one's thoughts and actions, brought immeasurable improvement to the Freedmen's quality of life.

Having an organized congregation and a church building for devotions led to new experiences and events sponsored by the church. One such example is the Grand Bush Meeting in 1898. Research indicates that the Bush meetings in the early 1900s were held to support the temperance movement to rid the country of alcohol. It appears, according to an advertisement in the *Washington Bee*, that First Baptist was eager to participate: "Grand Bush Meeting by the First Baptist Church of Merrifield, Fairfax County, Va., at Campbell's Grove, the third Sunday, July 18th (tomorrow). Trains will leave Sixth Street Depot at 9:00 a.m. and return at 8:40 p.m. Preaching every evening. Closing on Sunday night, July 25th. Round trip tickets, 50 cts."[132]

In the *Fairfax Herald* of August 3, 1900, an article was written, noting that

> [a]*bout 150 colored people collected at Merrifield on Wednesday evening of last week to celebrate the close of a four years' pastorate by Rev. Cornelius Wilson* [Williams]....*The chickens brought for sacrifice on this occasion numbered 150, or one for each adult present; 120 cakes were also contributed, and a very enjoyable time was had.*

Within church history, Reverend Wilson (or Williams) is listed as the first minister.[133] Reverend Williams was a valued asset to the church and was known for his firm guidance and decision-making abilities in determining what was beneficial for First Baptist. With the retirement of Reverend Williams, another pastor was called. On April 8, 1902, the *Washington Post* reported that the Salem Baptist Church's minister, Reverend J.D. Herbin, had resigned due to disagreements amongst the board of trustees and its members. Reverend Herbin was then called to pastor at First Baptist Church of Merrifield and assumed his pastoral duties, presumably in May 1902. Reverend J.D. Herbin was the second minister after Reverend Cornelius Williams to pastor at the church in Merrifield.[134] Unfortunately, it's unclear who was pastoring between the retirement of Reverend Williams and the installment of Reverend Herbin. Perhaps circuit ministers were providing the religious services and duties for the members. Further research into this area is warranted.

As the church expanded its fellowship, it also extended its reach into the community. A 1929 *Washington Post* article reported that the First Baptist Church of Merrifield was set to welcome the assistant to the president of Howard University, Reverend W. Stuart Nelson, as a speaker for the Fairfax Central Sunday School Union's thirty-ninth anniversary. The event was expected to draw more than one hundred Sunday school workers to the church's modest rural building.[135] David Honesty, an established Black family member from First Baptist Church of Vienna, proudly served as the organization's treasurer. From humble beginnings by congregants who worshiped in a log cabin, built a structure that was destroyed by weather and subsequently rebuilt, they were now hosting an event with a prestigious member of Howard University and one hundred Sunday school workers. This must have been a crowning point for this small group of parishioners and for a small church.

In 1959, First Baptist of Merrifield continued into the national realm of religion by joining the National Revival. The *Washington Post* reported:

> *The Baptist Churches of Washington Metropolitan Area are joining with Baptists throughout North America in a Simultaneous Revival Crusade during 1959 to bring you the word of God in all its dynamic power…the crusade will officially launch the Baptist Jubilee Advance which culminates in 1964 with the Sesquicentennial observance of organized Baptist work on our Continent.*

This campaign was not segregated, and many Baptist churches joined the efforts.

The "Old Church"

Black residents from the Merrifield area—along with the Pines, Ilda and Williamstown—joined First Baptist Church of Merrifield. One congregant was Viola Johnson-Richardson, who grew up in Ilda, attended the Merrifield Colored School and joined First Baptist. Viola and her sister Doris walked three miles one way to the church. My mother and Viola were close friends, and they sat at the mourner's bench together. They were baptized in the ice-filled Accotink together and worshiped together. Ms. Johnson-Richardson said that the time she spent at Merrifield was wonderful and worth the three-mile walk. Viola began attending Merrifield because her school was situated just across from the church. The faces were familiar, as she went to school with children who also attended First Baptist, and she knew almost all the adults in Merrifield.

Viola remembered how her mother bought a piano and invited Guy V. Collins from the Pines, who was also the Senior Choir director, to come to Ilda to teach Viola and her younger sister to play the piano. Collins was a man ahead of his time. He was the son of William Collins Jr. and the brother to my grandmother. He had spent a lifetime taking musical instruction from professors in Washington, D.C., and New York. There was no instrument that Guy could not play, but piano was his forte. Teaching piano and tuning them was how he provided for his family. On this day, while taking lessons, Guy told Viola and her sister about the Senior Choir. The sisters loved music and singing, so they joined the Senior Choir at Merrifield, although the rest of her family joined another church.

She remembered that "Uncle Joe" Collins, Guy's uncle, would sometimes pick her and her sister up for services at First Baptist, at least until her brother purchased a car. She admired the men at Merrifield—Guy V. Collins,

Photo of Viola Johnson-Richardson and her children. *Courtesy of author.*

Reverend Terry, Freddie Ransell, Clarence Gibson, Joseph Collins and Walter Hyson. Their deep love of God and community was more than honorable to her. She also held a special fondness for my grandmother and her sister, Myra, as well as Helen, both members of the Collins family.

Viola's memories of the "Old Church" were poignant. She spoke of learning to love and be loved by God. She talked about how the Collins and Lee families were a part of that learning experience. She was thankful for a space, like the church in Merrifield, because while worshiping she forgot the evils of segregation, which loomed outside the stained-glass windows. She was told by her father that "you had to know your place" when it came to White people. With Viola's passion for God, she joined the Baptist Youth Convention (BYC). She sang with the Crusaders, a group of Black folks from all the Black Baptist churches that sang under the guidance of Guy Collins. Each fifth Sunday a church in the Baptist Union would host a morning service, and the Crusaders sang. She also became the assistant superintendent for the church's Sunday school under the instructions of Walter Hyson, the superintendent.

Vividly lodged in my brain are the memories of the "Old Church." I lived right next to the building, which meant that my parents and I were always at religious services. In the 1960s, Freddie Ransell was the chairman of the Deacon Board. His predecessor was Mr. George Hyson, whose home was near the second "Colored School." I recall the entrance of the original church structure facing Porter Road, an unpaved path branching from Gallows Road. The building was modest in size yet inviting; its exterior was painted white, and the interior was a light shade of gray. Stained-glass windows adorned the church, and atop the roof sat a small steeple, with a bell that echoed during "watch meeting" services on New Year's Eve—a tradition rooted in the anticipation of emancipation on January 1, 1863, by those enslaved. My mother had told me the Bell that rang each New Years was purchased at Mr. Dunn's store. I have a memory of the wooden floors creaking as congregants tapped their feet to the rhythm of long-meter hymns. These hymns or melodies are sung without instrumental accompaniment.

First Baptist Church of Merrifield Senior Choir. *Courtesy of the author.*

The pews, crafted from dark wood, bore the marks of extensive use and were unforgivingly firm. Concrete steps led to the white front door. Upon opening the door, you would find yourself in a small vestibule, which could accommodate no more than three or four people. If you were late for morning service, you had to wait until the ushers opened the doors to the sanctuary, allowing you to find a seat.

At the front of the church stood a brown table designated for the bread and wine during Sunday Communion. Behind it was a raised platform, dark in color, with wooden rails outlining the area where the pastor would deliver sermons. Beyond the pulpit lay the modest yet sufficient choir gallery, bathed in the sparkling hues of stained glass on sunny days. At the heart of the choir space was an organ played by Deacon Guy V. Collins for the Senior Choir. Off to the right was the choir room, where the black robes with white sashes were stored. The back of the building on the left side was a small office for the pastor. The original structure of Merrifield lacked a designated pulpit and choir gallery. It wasn't until the early '40s when Seth Williams, a member of the community and creator of Williamstown, constructed the addition at the rear of the building, complete with a pulpit and choir stand.

Initially, the church was warmed by a potbellied stove, but during my childhood, we benefited from direct heat via a furnace located in the basement. In the 1960s, the building lacked air conditioning, making the humid and oppressive summer months quite challenging. Our sole respite was the cool breeze that flowed through the open windows, complemented by the shade provided by the grand walnut and pine trees. Paper fans, which advertised a funeral home, were another method to combat the heat.

Photo of the interior of the original First Baptist Church of Merrifield at the church and pastor anniversary. *Courtesy of Robert "Bobbi" Whitmore.*

Naturally, the effectiveness of the fan depends on the speed of your fanning. With no indoor plumbing available, all bathroom needs were directed to the outhouse. An outhouse was located on the boundary line between my house and the church. But since I had running water and a functional bathroom, I skipped the outhouse and just walked across the yard to use my own.

Black people who lived in Merrifield and the surrounding area used the church for worship, a time of fellowship from the harshness of racism and bigotry. W.E.B. Du Bois claimed, "From such beginnings arose and spread with marvelous rapidity, the Negro church, the first distinctively Negro American social institution."[136] After emancipation it "represented both the institutionalization of Black community life and defiance to white authority. They [Blacks] turned to the church for cultural, social, and recreational as well as spiritual needs."[137] First Baptist was a perfect example of Du Bois's viewpoint. On any given Sunday, there could be three services: one at approximately 11:30 a.m., another at 3:30 p.m. and a third at 7:00 p.m. Plays and pageants were regularly organized. Annual events such as Homecoming, Revival and Rally Day have been generational traditions since the church's inception. During my mother's youth, the church was linked to the Merrifield Colored School across the street. Most of the schoolchildren attended First Baptist, so pageants, recitals and other activities were joint endeavors between the school and the church. It was necessary for these activities to be organized in the one-room schoolhouse and presented in the church, as the Merrifield Colored School could not accommodate large assemblies.

I have a clear recollection of a play titled *Heaven's Gate*, presented by the Senior Choir and performed in the old sanctuary in the early 1960s. The plot centered on the newly deceased arriving at the heavenly gate, where entry was granted if their name appeared in the Book of Life. With their name entered, they were allowed into Heaven to be with God. Those not listed were denied access. The Devil, on the other hand, would confront each soul en route to the gate, tempting them with wine and women in an effort to luring them to Hell. The Devil promised the newly dead that all their desires would be fulfilled. The choir members were all dressed in white robes with silver crowns. The small pulpit area and choir gallery was transformed into a heavenly space where a soul could rest in the glory of God. This performance was done in the old church and in the new one as well. These are the personal memories of my experiences within the walls of the old and new church.

In my day, I was baptized in the baptismal pool in the basement of the new church. Unlike my mother, I did not have to go the mourner's bench and ask for forgiveness. I simply told Reverend Charles Parker that I believed in Christ. However, in my mother's youth, baptism was a cold affair. Because of no running water in the old church, congregants were taken to the banks of the Accotink bridge and dipped in the name of the Father and of the Son and of the Holy Spirit. The waters of the Accotink ran under Woodburn Road, and in the winter, it was extremely challenging for baptisms, as the frigid weather caused the creek to ice over. The deacons, being resourceful,

First Baptist Church of Merrifield, 1972. *Digital Collection for Fairfax County Library, Adolph Brice Collection.*

chipped away at the ice to have a place for the pastor to perform the ceremony. My mother was dipped in the cold Accotink and was taken back by horse and wagon to the church for fellowship. She said that to her knowledge, no one ever became sick or died from the dip in the cold Accotink.

Routinely, services in the church started with devotion. Freddie Ransell, as the lead deacon, would open the floor for people to speak about the goodness of the Lord. This is when anyone and everyone got up to testify about God's grace. As a child, I knew that it was not over until Deacon Ransell got up and said his prayer of loving the Lord until his head hit his dying pillow. It is hard to believe, but most services lasted two and a half hours, except on Communion Sunday, which was the first Sunday of the month; it seemed like you were in church for a lifetime.

Other parishioners my age have thoughtful memories of the old church. Traveling down Porter Road, passing my house and then turning to the right leads you to the home of twins Darlene and Charlene Terry. Like myself, these twins were raised in Merrifield, attended First Baptist and were baptized by Reverend Charles R. Parker. Reverend Parker had the longest tenure of all the ministers. He served Merrifield church faithfully from 1941 to 1973. I share fond childhood memories of the old Baptist church with Charlene and Darlene Terry. I remember that their mother and father,

Aaron and Shirley Terry, were fixtures in the church and the community. Aaron, who was Freddie Ransell's nephew, was held in such high esteem by Freddie that when he resigned as chairman of the Deacon Board, he confidently nominated Aaron for the role.

The Terry twins have a remarkable collective memory of the old church. Charlene recalled a small wooden structure separate from the church, with a glass-less opening used as a serving window. The wooden building, located in the churchyard, sold dinners to raise money for a building fund to construct a new church. However, it is easy to surmise that the dinners were also sold because there were no restaurants that would serve Black people after the long church services. The only diner in Merrifield was Harvey's at the intersection of Lee Highway and Gallows Road, and it was strictly segregated. However, it is noted that while White customers could bring in their dogs to the lunch counter, Blacks were forbidden from entering.

Both twins remembered the church's interior and those who contributed to its services, including Reverend Parker and Reverend Pearson at the pulpit, and their father, Aaron Terry, who was among the executive board officers of First Baptist. The Terry family, who lived just down the road from me, have been an integral part of Merrifield's story for many years and continue to worship at First Baptist. Their family's land is now home to a business complex. It must be noted that Aaron Terry's parents, the twins' grandmother and grandfather, Everett and Edith Terry, lived next to the old church on the side facing Gallows Road. A service station has been built on this site.

Early in its history, the church's congregation grew. It became a vital source of religious and educational guidance within the community. As told to me by my mother, Eulala, the early pioneering families of Merrifield included the Collins, Ransell, Robinsons, Lee, Bland, Hyson, Bradley, Terrys, Gibson, Blackwell, Fishes, Turner, Strother, Woodland, Locket, Ball, Pearson, Steward and Dixon families. According to my grandmother, the people of the Black community helped one another through challenging times. This is evident though the "pound parties" held often during the year. At these gatherings, church members would each bring a pound of something they could afford to share. For instance, one might bring a pound of butter from their dairy cows or a pound of cornmeal if their corn harvest was plentiful. Items were not purchased but rather exchanged within the group to support other families, particularly during the Great Depression. Although the church's footprint was small, the parishioners' hearts and compassion were immeasurable.

Photo of children's choir at the old First Baptist Church of Merrifield. Pictured in the first row, center, are Charlene and Darlene Terry. The last child on the first row is Norma Gordon. Ms. Rena Tayler is pictured in the back row, last on the right.

Avonjeanette spoke of a time when her grandmother Betty Collins sewed suits for a family whose father had died. Betty Collins was an example of how the church and its members came together to assist one another at times of need. In this case, it was five suits for five sons who grieved their father. Avonjeanette said, "There was a family in the Pines who had five boys and one girl; it was the Turner family. And the father used to work at the Stone Quarry and he got sick and he passed, and so the boys, you know they weren't rich, so the boys didn't have a suit to wear to their father's funeral. And my grandmother Betty gathered up all the suits that the men no longer wore because they were too small or whatever and with the pedal sewing machine, she made those five suits for those boys before the funeral."[138]

Photo of Betsy Williams-Collins, date unknown. *Courtesy of author.*

A bright spot in the church's history was the Sunday School Trip, which happened once a year in the summer months. It was to either Sparrows or Carl's beach in Annapolis, Maryland, or a northern city amusement park like Atlantic City or Wildwood, New Jersey. This one-day outing was our family's vacation. Like the other members of the Sunday school and church, this was important to us. My cousins and I bought new clothes for the day. Our mothers packed an ice chest with sodas. We never left without fried chicken and hardboiled eggs. Little did I know that these delicacies came from years of segregation and having to use the *Green Book* to find restaurants and hotels that would serve Black people. These two beaches in Maryland and the Atlantic Ocean in New Jersey were the only places we visited because Ocean City, Maryland, and white southern beaches south were off limits to African Americans.

Reverend Charles L. Parker

The longest-tenured minister at First Baptist was Reverend C.L. Parker. Reverend Parker was small in stature but large in his love of God and First Baptist of Merrifield. Parker was so dedicated to the church that he would commute from his home in Anacostia each Sunday, as well as during the week for church meetings and prayer services. The reverend would catch the bus from Washington, D.C., head toward Tremont Gardens (National Cemetery currently) and walk uphill for several miles to reach the church. When members realized that Parker was walking from Tremont, they began picking him up at the bus stop, driving him to the church and, after services, taking him home to Anacostia.

Photo of Reverend Charles L. Parker, First Baptist Church of Merrifield, 1950s. *Courtesy of Robert "Bobbi" Whitmore.*

Building a New Church Home

Reverend Parker was an inexhaustible leader, and with his guidance, the small but resolute church members embarked on a new endeavor to build a larger house of worship. With an estimated thirty-two active members, it all began in 1952, when a foundation was dug for the new building. This foundation was structured to be multi-functional, with walls and a roof so the worshipers could use it as a fellowship hall. It took years to finish construction of the first-floor sanctuary.

The build-out of the top floor was a community project and a labor of love. People like Robert Whitmore, who was one of the first Black mailmen in the area; Willie Lambert; William Nokes; Freddie Ransell; Avon Terry; Seth Williams; and many others gave up weekends to construct the new church building. They poured concrete, put cinder blocks in place, bricked up the front of the building, created walls and painted the building white. Freddie Ransell, a carpenter by trade, built kitchen cabinets, top and bottom. Mr. Lambert, a professional painter, used his abilities to paint the church, and William Nokes, who delivered bricks for a living, delivered bricks for the new church.

White residents, including D.A. Foster, the head of a construction company on Gallows Road, contributed significantly. Foster used his crane to place the rafters for the new building's roof. Other members gave what they could monetarily. The vision was clear: a larger church with running water, a fellowship hall, kitchen, choir galleries and classrooms. Members were determined to see the project through by using their God-given talents and fundraising abilities. Finally, thirteen years later—with prayer, devotion, chicken dinners and pageants, along with the apron fund and a buy-a-brick program, the parishioners walked into the new sanctuary in 1966. From 1941 until his death in 1973, Reverend Parker was the leader of the flock at the First Baptist Church of Merrifield. In 1965, Reverend C.L. Parker proudly

Photo of the original First Baptist Church of Merrifield, May 1958. On the left side of the church is the first floor of the new church under construction. *Courtesy of author.*

led the procession into the new church, and to this day, the church holds Sunday morning services along with other programs and events. Following is a list of the other ministers who led the church:

- Reverend Cornelius Williams
- Reverend J.D. Herbin
- Reverend B.S. Askew
- Reverend W.R. Manley
- Reverend Richard J. Carter
- Reverend Henry S. Washington
- Reverend Charles L. Parker (1941–73)
- Reverend William Dyson
- Reverend Eugene D. Terry (interim)
- Reverend Lenwood Graham Sr.
- Reverend Keith D. Kitchen
- Reverend Martin T. Pickett
- Reverend Kenny Smith
- Reverend Paul Sheppard

Opposite: Photo of First Baptist Church of Merrifield under construction, 1966. *Courtesy of author.*

Right: Photo of the march into the new church building for the First Baptist Church of Merrifield, 1966. Reverend Charles L. Parker is presiding, and Reverend Terry and Mrs. E. Terry are following. *Courtesy of author.*

After Reverend Parker's death in 1972, First Baptist Merrifield began to have conflict, and many churchgoers left the church home that they and their families had helped to create. Part of the problem was that a new world was opening around this once rural worship center. In the 1970s and 1980s, First Baptist became a neighbor to new homes, businesses and industrial complexes, forcing Merrifield to morph into an unrecognizable community. By the late 1970s, most of the Black people who once called Merrifield their home had moved—except for Deacon Freddie Ransell, who lived on his property next to the church until 1985. Ransell Road, which is now used as the main entrance road, was named after Chairman of the Deacon Board Freddie Ransell. The Merrifield area in the late '60s and '70s became an industrial dumping ground, with towing and welding companies, heavy equipment sites, warehouses and storefronts. It presented itself not as the residential mecca I remembered, but rather as an area lacking families and the familiarity in which I had group up.

In the late '70s and '80s, new folks came to the area. There came new members such as Loston and Armetia Harris; Reverend Vernon Pettius and his wife, Sue; and Reverend Clarence Brown and his wife, Hattie, along with the return of Pauline Gray, whose mother was Edith Collins-Terry. Pauline had become a widow after the loss of her husband, Reverend Charles Gray; she had been the first lady at Second Baptist in Clifton, Virginia. New clubs

Photo of original First Baptist Church of Merrifield building prior to its demolition, 1970s. *Courtesy of author.*

were added to the church, including the Nurses Unit and Golden Agers, and a preschool was developed in the Charles Parker Fellowship Hall. New choirs were formed, such as the Junior Chorus, directed by Theresa Wells and Reverend Velma Massenburg, along with the Spiritual Melodies, directed by Avonjeanette Hill.

The elders I remember have mostly passed away. There are a few still living, and one is 106 years old. The church looks much as it did when we marched inside on that sunny day in 1966. The outside is painted white, and the original footprint and structure of the building have not changed. But there is an addition to the roofline, with a cross. The church bell, which once hung proudly in the old church steeple, is now out front on a brick edifice where congregants and visitors can view it. The wooden kitchen cabinets that Freddie Ransell made from scratch are still in place in the church kitchen, and the bricks that were laid along the sidewalk pathway are still there. What is missing is the energetic neighborhood that surrounded the church—the people of color who worked hard, came to worship in their Sunday best and took care of one another like good neighbors should. At least I still have those memories.

CHAPTER 8

SONS AND DAUGHTERS OF LIBERTY LODGE

Pound parties and pageants were not enough to provide a barrier between the injustice of segregation and racism. On March 4, 1907, to augment the safety net necessary for Black people within Fairfax and the Providence District, the men of Merrifield established a lodge. At the corner of Porter and Gallows Road, Robert Bradley sold free and simple land to the trustees of the Grand Order of the Sons and Daughters of Liberty Lodge of America. The trustees—Robert Bradley, John Coates, Charles V. Hyson, Joshua Ball and Joshua Pearson—laid the cornerstone.[139] Another trustee of the hall was Charles H. Tinner, a landowner in Merrifield who purchased five and three-fourths acres off Gallows Road in 1904.[140] The Tinners were a prominent African American family who were instrumental in the establishment of the community of Falls Church. Today, you can learn more about the Tinner family history through the Tinner Hill Foundation and the park that has been established in their honor.

The narrative of Liberty Lodge and its service to the Merrifield community must be viewed from many levels. Primarily, it was an organization for the men that provided a sense of agency within a society that viewed them as second-class citizens. Most importantly, it was a way to aid people of color and their families as they navigated life through challenging waters of segregation.[141] The lodge also found a solution to a problem. Merrifield needed land to bury its dead. Cemeteries were, not surprisingly, segregated, and a stipulation in the church deed firmly stated that the First Baptist Church of Merrifield could not place a cemetery on the property. Once again, African Americans found a way to circumvent the restrictions and provide a permanent place to bury their loved ones.

According to historical accounts, the cemetery was established in 1907, when Mr. Richard Slaughter, a landowner in the Pines, sold a 1.25-acre parcel to Liberty Lodge for use as a graveyard.[142] In total, Mr. Slaughter owned 5.5 acres of land and sold the 1.25 acres to the Grand United Order of the Sons and Daughters of Liberty Lodge No. 14 for seventy-five dollars. Avonjeanette recounted that in order to reach Liberty Cemetery, a hearse had to travel over a rickety wooden bridge to cross Slaughters Spring. The eerie creaks of the bridge as the hearse passed over were quite haunting. Today, the spring is gone, the bridge no longer exists and the entrance to the cemetery has been relocated; it seems that nothing of the Pines remains visible or in its original place.

The Liberty Lodge Cemetery was in use for years. My mother said that during Memorial Day, families would gather at the cemetery to clear away weeds and debris. After placing flowers to honor their dead, the families would sit down for a picnic meal. This ritual passed from generation to generation until 1965.

Photo of the Liberty Lodge Cemetery with the black fence, 2000s. *Courtesy of author.*

However, things changed in 1965. The Fairfax County School Board decided to use eminent domain to acquire twenty-two acres of land in the Pines neighborhood, including the Liberty Lodge Cemetery, to build a new, desegregated high school. This new school would have replaced the segregated Luther Jackson High School in Merrifield. After years without higher-level educational institutions for African Americans, the board opened Luther Jackson High School in 1954 for all Black students in the county. After desegregation, Luther Jackson was converted into an intermediate school. This action forced the African American community of the Pines to surrender their land within sixty days to the Fairfax County School Board. Despite the forceful legal measures to acquire and demolish their homes, the surrendered land remained undeveloped for decades.

The devastating plan to displace Black families, the dissolution of a community and, most tragically, the absence of the promised school culminated in significant loss of land that had been nurtured and valued by people of color for generations. To add insult to injury, the board allowed Mobil Oil Company, which was building its corporate headquarters on Gallows Road, to dump the dirt from the construction site onto Collins's old property. However, the worst part of this tragedy is the promises made by the Fairfax County School Board to maintain the Liberty Lodge Cemetery so family members could still visit and remember their dead. This did not happen for decades. I remember in the '70s listening to my grandmother's heartbreak about losing the land her father had given her and then experiencing the inability to visit her grandfather's and mother's graves. She mourned this loss until the day she died.

A *Fairfax Journal* article dated May 5, 1998, noted, "Ronald Marshall was riding his horse in the woods near Woodburn Road in Merrifield where his great-grandfather's farm once stood [William H. Collins Jr.]. There in the woods called the Pines, he discovered the graves of his ancestors hidden among the undergrowth, their headstones toppled by vandals."[143] It was clear that from 1965 until the 1990s, the county had defaulted on its promise to preserve and maintain the Liberty Cemetery. Among the weeds buried in the soil of the Pines are the remains of more than forty to fifty pioneers of the Black Merrifield community. William Collins Sr. and Jennie Ransell's infant children are there, along with Betty Collins. The only tombstone to survive the neglect is that of Betty Collins, who died on January 9, 1920. Guy Collins, Betty's son, was also quoted in the *Fairfax Journal* article saying, "So many are buried there who don't have any stones."[144] He also remarked, "The cemetery is all that's left of life in the Pines."[145] Guy was the last remaining member of the Liberty Lodge organization but has since passed away on February 11, 1999.

In the 1990s, due to persistent pressure from the families and following an NBC interview with my grandmother Myra, along with articles about the cemetery, the school board took steps to fulfill its maintenance obligations for the grave sites. The school board cleared the debris, cleaned up the cemetery and placed a black fence around the perimeter. In an act of decency, the board also hired the Smithsonian to use tomography imaging over the property to locate graves. To complete this saga, in the early 2000s I met an individual who was on the project to find my ancestors' resting places. He was such a nice man and so proud that he could help my family. It was serendipitous that I met him. Perhaps the ancestors wanted me to say thank you.

To this day, there is still no school, and the cemetery is surrounded by a forty-two-acre park named Pine Ridge Park. Through a land swap, the school board sold the land to the park authority, and now soccer fields and community gardens grace the grounds of my ancestors' historical property. However, a blacktop road exists, courtesy of the park authority, that leads to the cemetery's front gate. Beyond the chain link fence stands a sign paying tribute to the veterans and numerous citizens known to rest there. Eagle Scouts and family members often return to the graves to clear leaves and lay flowers. Although the members of the Sons and Daughters of the Liberty Lodge have all passed away and the organization no longer exists, their descendants continue the Memorial Day traditions, cleaning the property and breaking bread together. A debt of gratitude must go to Hareem Badil-Abish, who tirelessly worked to ensure that the Liberty Cemetery was restored and preserved for future generations. Unfortunately, Hareem has passed away, but he was laid to rest in the cemetery he fought so hard to reconstruct.

The Odd Fellows Hall

For $100, land was purchased by Seth Williams, Charles Harrison Tinner and John Phillips, all trustees of the Blue Ridge Lodge No. 8500, Grand United Order of Odd Fellows in America. This land was to be used for a permanent structure in Merrifield, Virginia, for their hall.[146] The Order of Odd Fellows was built in association with the First Baptist Church of Merrifield, with both structures being constructed near each other on Gallows Road. Williams, Tinner and Phillips were trustees of Merrifield

Right: Photo of the Odd Fellows Hall converted into Boyd's Pianos. The building has been demolished. *Courtesy of author*.

Below: Cornerstone of Blue Ridge Lodge No. 8500, Grand United Order of the Odd Fellows No. 1938 and Naomi Household of Ruth, September 30, 1917. *Courtesy of author.*

and for the Order of Odd Fellows.[147] Tinner was a member of the Tinner family in Falls Church who organized to protest the ordinance for segregated neighborhoods in the area. Tinner also was elected a member of a road improvement group representing the Black community.[148] Within the September 9, 1927 edition of the *Fairfax Herald*, Tinner and his group requested road improvements in the area surrounding the Merrifield Colored School.[149] Notably, the Tinner family have been advocates for change in the Black communities for decades.

The Grand United Order of Odd Fellows (GUOOF) in the United States was founded in 1843 as a mutual aid and fraternal organization. Initially established to provide support for disenfranchised African Americans, the Odd Fellows served as a charitable institution dedicated to assisting widows, the ill and individuals with disabilities, as well as offering burial assistance. Furthermore, the organization functioned as a social club and allowed Blacks to utilize its building for various purposes. It operated as a movie theater and a night school for African Americans pursuing vocational training, including cosmetology, and it also served as an overflow school during the late 1930s. A distinctive strength of this organization was its commitment to the principles of temperance and integrity.

However, the GUOOF cannot be confused with the White institution, as Whites refused to allow the establishment of a Black Odd Fellows chapter. As early as 1819, African American men in Baltimore were wanting to establish but were refused a charter. Because of the inability to create their own lodge within the American order, Black men turned to England and its Grand United Order of Odd Fellows. It is believed that the organization had its roots in England. This attempt for a charter was spearheaded by Peter Ogden, a Black ship steward who traveled frequently between New York and Liverpool. In 1843, these men were granted a Grand United Order of Odd Fellows through England.[150]

In 1984, the hall in Merrifield was purchased and repurposed as a piano showroom, where a white grand piano sat in the upper-level window on display for years. They maintained this space to sell pianos until 2016, when the property was purchased and the building demolished. I wanted to purchase the building and turn it into a museum, but I couldn't afford the $10 million price tag. I did, however, take pictures of the original flooring and stovepipe cover, along with the exterior, interior and cornerstone of the structure.

HOUSEHOLD OF RUTH

The Grand United Order in Merrifield also had a women's membership group, the Household of Ruth, which was established as an extension to the male-only Odd Fellows. As time progressed, wives felt the need for a woman's auxiliary to coincide with the work their husbands were doing within the community. Its charter granted "wife, mother or daughter as a contributing member and be benefited thereby. Hence, from such desires, the Household of Ruth was formed. Its role was simple, to extend and encourage friendships, boost truths and disperse love throughout the community." Several years ago, while researching another topic, I spotted a receipt for a payment made to the Household of Ruth by Jennie Collins-Ransell for monthly dues. Unfortunately, I did not make a copy of the receipt, but I am still searching documents or minutes pertaining to the Merrifield chapter.[151]

Chapter 9

THE PINES

The Pines, named for the abundant pine trees that blanket the area, represent a rich extension of the Merrifield community. By the early 1900s, this vibrant enclave was home to notable families, including William H. Collins Jr. and Sr., Douglas Collins, Jennie Collins-Ransell, William Robinson, Jerry Robinson, Vernard Ransell, Clarence Ransell, Willie Robinson, Elburn Collins, Joseph Collins, Norman Collins, Steven Fish and Richard Slaughter. Historical land deeds reveal that William H. Collins Jr. was the first resident of this Black community, acquiring his property in 1905. Following his lead, other families, like the Slaughters, settled in the area, strengthening the community's foundation. Many families were devoted members of the First Baptist Church of Merrifield and ensured that their children and grandchildren attended the Merrifield Colored School, fostering a sense of continuity and belonging. The close-knit nature of these families, many of whom had roots in Falls Church or the Gravel Bank near Shreve Road, created a supportive and enduring legacy in this significant community.

In 2001, a memo written by Richard Saachi of the Fairfax County Park Authority noted that the land where the Pines once thrived was held by the Fitzhugh and Chichester families during the eighteenth and nineteenth centuries. These families were not only slave owners but also farmers, operating mills and owning extensive properties in the region. Historical records later revealed that Mary Mason, the wife of James Mason, and Henrietta Clows became owners of this land. In 1890, a significant land dispute culminated in Mary Mason acquiring 85 acres, a settlement that marked a pivotal moment in history. This acquisition gave rise to what is now known as the "Mason Tract." Furthermore, a deed from 1905 belonging to William Collins Jr. confirms his ownership of 5.5 acres, further solidifying the importance of the "Mason Tract" in the community's heritage.[152]

William Jr.'s property was situated along what is now known as Woodburn Road, directly behind the Fairfax Hospital Medical Complex. Simply put, in 1905, the establishment of this neighborhood can be traced back to William Jr. and his father, William H. Collins Sr., along with Richard Slaughter in 1906. These three men moved onto the Mason Tract and founded a community for their families known as the Pines.

William H. Collins Sr.

Prior to lots in the Mason Tract being sold to African Americans, it was an unoccupied wooded landscape of rocky soil. Nevertheless, there are three individuals who are looked on as the founders of the Pines. One is William H. Collins Sr. Although William Sr.'s background is complex, it has been surmised he was enslaved. It is said that Collins's father, Wallace Collins, was the son of a White man named John Collins who enslaved William's mother, Sarah. However, further research is needed, as oral histories provided by my mother, Eulala, and my aunt offer a different perspective. The information on William Sr.'s grave marker is not disputed; it states that his mother was Matilda Grady and that his father was Wallace Collins. These two facts are confirmed. My mother often spoke about her grandfather William Collins Sr. She mentioned that he enjoyed sitting and listening to her read books that he purchased from the Salvation Army. He also shared stories about his life, claiming that he was Native American. He recounted that when he was young, he was forced to go to Oklahoma, but as soon as he could, he escaped and *walked back* to the Washington, D.C. area. He often shared tales about his experiences and his life to my mother.

William H. Collins Sr. was born in 1843, during the time of the Native American Removal Act. He also was alive when Virginia adopted laws against interracial marriage and declared that Native Americas were to be listed on the census as "Black," "Negro" or "Mulatto." In 1924, the Virginia Assembly implemented the Racial Integrity Act. It was spearheaded by the head of the Virginia Vital Statistics, who was a White supremacist named Walter Plecker. Plecker, who was also a eugenicist, pushed for the enforcement of racial segregation—no interracial marriages, and persons living in Virginia as Native would have to identify on paper as either White or Black. Furthermore, if you were previously listed as Native on a birth certificate, it was changed. To make matters worse, in Virginia during the 1920s, if you claimed to be Native it could result in your imprisonment. This might explain why William Collins Sr. only confided this information to a few individuals, leading to a limited number of people who were aware of his Native heritage.

My mother, Eulala Lee-Ransell, was extremely close to her grandfather, whom she affectionately called "Grand-Pa Collins." She always maintained that he had Native American heritage. Collins's use of the phrase "walked back" is significant, as Dr. Gabriel Tayac, a Piscataway Native and professor at George Mason University for Indigenous Studies, has noted hearing this phrase among other Natives, making Collins's heritage worth investigating. My mother also mentioned that their White neighbors were fearful of Grandpa because of his Indigenous background and his keen abilities with horses. To be honest, little is known about the probability of my great-great-grandfather's Indigenous roots, and currently no historical documents, such as a slave schedule, are available to confirm or deny whether Collins was enslaved. The only tangible evidence comes from oral history accounts and DNA results. The great-granddaughter of William Sr., Avonjeannette Lee-Hill, has DNA matching the Saponi and Powhatan Native American tribes. Additionally, Avonjeanette' s niece, my first cousin Denise Bonds-Allen, has had her DNA certified as matching Powhatan DNA as well, and I share the same DNA results. Despite the DNA findings, many questions may never be answered. For example, if Collins were Saponi, why did he go to Oklahoma? Why would he walk back? I also did not find any slave schedules that would support the theory that Collins's mother and father were enslaved. While I am not dismissing the possibility of enslavement or his Indigenous roots, what I am saying is there needs to be further research into Collins's ancestry.

We have some knowledge about the Saponi tribe, primarily through the history of Thomas Collins, an early frontiersman whose family intermarried with Saponi Native Americans. Tom Collins's lineage includes several males named John Collins. Given this information, could the White enslaver named John Collins be mistaken for John Collins from the Saponi tribe? It is historically documented that the Saponi tribe lived, for a time, at Fort Christiana, a historic site located in what is now Lawrenceville, Virginia. The fort, constructed in 1714 by order of Virginia's Governor Alexander Spotswood, was built for the protection of White settlers and friendly Native tribes, like the Saponins. Although the fort was decommissioned in 1717, the tribe continued to live in and around the fortification. The Saponi tribe has a long history of movement from place to place, sometimes living near Charlottesville or Louisa County in Virginia, along with North Carolina, New York and Tennessee. It's important to note the proximity of Louisa County to Henrico County and Richmond, where it is believed William was born. There is only a fifty-four-mile difference between them. Because of this, it is possible that William Sr. lived in or around these areas.

These inconsistencies highlight the need for further DNA analysis, especially the work being done by Thomas Lutz Allen, who has twenty-five years of expertise in genealogy. Additional investigation into local archives in Henrico, Surry and surrounding counties near Richmond is also necessary. Furthermore, examining the interpretation of "walk back," along with the potential presence of the Saponi's in Oklahoma and local tribal data, would be significant.

Regardless, before relocating to the Pines, William Sr. enlisted into the U.S. Colored Troops on December 13, 1863. He was in the First U.S. Colored Calvary (USCT), which was organized on May 19, 1863, in Washington, D.C. He was stationed in the Portsmouth and Yorktown area of Virginia but did go as far as North Carolina.[153] After the war, William was noted in the 1870 census as living in Falls Church on Samuel Fish's farm. William became acquainted with Fish during the Civil War, when the two men served together. Fish's Uncle, Henry Fish, also lived on the farm, along with Fish's daughter Mariah (or Maria) Tabertha Fish. It is through this relationship with Samuel that William meets and marries Mariah Fish in 1871. Later, he is recorded on the 1880 census as living in Alexandria with his wife Mariah Tabertha Collins, and his children: Martha, age nine; William H. Jr., age six; and Douglas, age three.[154] There were several other children, including Norman and Joseph Collins.

William Sr. moved again to the Gravel Bank in the Providence District of Fairfax County. Unfortunately, by 1895, William had become a widower. But in 1899, he was registered as having another wife, named Hatty Bell Huduall of Fauquier County, Virginia. William and Hatty had three children: Ruth, Theodore and Gladys. There is confusion surrounding the wives of William Sr. Some family members believe that Mariah (Maria) and Tabertha were two different individuals. However, based on my research and the oral histories passed down from my mother and Avonjeanette Hill, I believe they are the same person. Some research indicates that both Tabertha and Mariah died in the same year, 1895, which supports my theory. In 1870, William was living with the Fishes. His marriage license states that he married Mariah

(Maria) in 1871. By 1880, he was residing in Alexandria's Freedman's Village with Tabertha and their three children. Although I was unable to find the 1890 census, by 1900, William Collins had married Hattie Bell Huduall.

William H. Collins Jr.

Photo of William H. Collins Jr. in his yard in the Pines. *Courtesy of author.*

William H. Collins Jr. was born in 1875 in Fairfax County, Virginia, to Mariah and William Sr. In 1880, when he was a young child, he lived with his parents and two siblings in Freedman's Village in Alexandria, Virginia. In 1896, William joined the military as a Buffalo Soldier. According to family oral history, he was an excellent equestrian and was regarded as a "horse whisperer." This skill may have influenced his decision to join the Tenth Cavalry, Troop C. During his service, William was deployed to various locations in the western United States, where he fought against local Native American tribes. However, in 1898, he was sent to Cuba, where he participated in battles at Santiago and San Juan Hill. These battles were significant in demonstrating the bravery and capabilities of the Buffalo Soldiers. Utilizing warfare tactics learned from Indigenous people, the Buffalo Soldiers played a crucial role in securing victories. Without their expert military skills, Theodore Roosevelt and his Rough Riders might have faced defeat in these engagements.

After returning from war on October 12, 1899, William married Betsy Elizabeth Williams. Earlier, Betsy's mother, Jennie, had met and married Charles C. Steward after she was emancipated from slavery. Jennie is a fascinating figure in Collins family history, as it is believed that Charles Steward, Betsy's father, was a physician in Washington, D.C. It is said he practiced at the "Dispensary and Emergency Hospital" at 1711 New York Avenue, NW. When I was growing up, the elders always said that Dr. Steward was Betsy's stepfather; however, DNA results prove that Charles C. Steward was Betsy's biological father. Additionally, genealogical research indicates that Charles's parents were Daniel Collins, a White farmer in Virginia, and his wife, Eliza Hieronimus, who also was White. Charles Steward was White, practiced medicine at a local hospital and was married to a formerly enslaved woman, who then gave birth to a mixed-race daughter named Betsy. My grandmother Myra spoke about visiting her grandmother Jennie in D.C. She said that her home was beautiful and had stained-glass windows. Unfortunately, Dr. Steward died young, and as the story goes, his family were not fond of Jennie. To survive after her husband's death, she opened a candy shop in her home in the District of Columbia.

Richard Slaughter

Richard Slaughter purchased his Mason Tract one year after William H. Collins Jr. Slaughter, born in 1838, was a Virginia native who could have been enslaved. In the 1900 census, he is listed as married to Rosetta, or Rosa Slaughter, with two children, Charles and Emma Slaughter. Slaughter, along with Collins, are listed as enrolling their children in the Merrifield Colored School when it opened. Like Collins, the Slaughters' livelihood was rooted within the soil of the Pines. Many of these families were truck farmers, growing fruits and vegetables to sustain their households and sell at the Washington, D.C. markets.

In her oral history, Avonjeanette Lee-Hill mentioned that her grandfather William Collins Jr. had a home office. On Mondays, he used the space to tie up loose ends from the previous Saturday's market. He then started the preparations for the following weekend's sales downtown. On the Collins farm, they raised chickens, geese, cows and pigs and had a fruit orchard, as well as rows of corn and other vegetables. My grandmother Myra told me when the Depression hit, they did not go hungry because they grew plenty of food to feed the family. From their summer crops, they canned and preserved vegetables and smoked meat. However, she also mentioned some White families were not as fortunate with food. These families would receive assistance from her grandfather because this was the heart and soul of the Pines and their inhabitants. It was a community that saw no color, just humanity.

The Pines didn't have electricity until after World War II, and when the weather became cool, the men would gather and participate in hog killing. Not having electricity or refrigeration, this was a necessity for survival, as pork was easy to preserve and provided meat through the long winter months. Even so, my mother hated this time of year because the men got drunk and the women did all the cleaning of the meats. I assume this is why my grandmother did not like alcohol, and I never saw a bottle of spirits or beer in her home. I believe that some of her disdain for the drinking of liquor was due to the hog-killing experience. But hog-killing time and lacking electricity weren't the only hardships the residence of the Pines experienced. When water was needed, the children would have to go down to Slaughters Spring and get buckets to bring back to their homes. Many times, it was said there may be a snake or two looming around the creek bed, so great care was taken not to get bitten.

Photo of Elburn Collins during hog killing time in the Pines. To the right is a person named Robert, but his last name is unknown. *Courtesy of author.*

But there were respites of fun. Avonjeanette mentioned playing a game where they threw a ball over their house roof, with children on the other side waiting to catch it. The other children would then throw the ball back. Baseball was always a favorite, along with boxing and horseshoe throwing. However, the main source of entertainment was music. My grandmother and grandfather both played the piano, and they had a beautiful cherry wood upright piano to practice on. Granddad was an exceptional musician, and he made extra money by performing in Jutt-Joints playing ragtime tunes.

Singing was also part of family fun. All of Myra's children could sing and knew how to read music. On Sundays they sang in the choir, and any occasion was a good excuse to gather around the piano to hum a tune. In wintertime, they skated on frozen ponds, sled down slippery slopes of farmland or made clothes out of feed sacks. It is also known that Myra raised prize chickens—not chickens to eat, as some were considered quite rare. She saw them as pets.

When William Collins Jr. passed away in 1953, his children—Myra Lee, Helen Marshall, Roscoe, Guy and Elburn Collins—inherited his property. They each had their own homes within the community of the Pines. Helen and Myra lived side by side, and Guy's house faced Woodburn Road. Elburn

Photo of the Pines, 1940s. *Courtesy of author.*

and Roscoe lived in between the sisters and Guy. Two of William Jr.'s children, Hatten and Raymond, both died during infancy and our buried at the Sons and Daughters Liberty Lodge Cemetery.

During World War II, Roscoe developed an eye issue that caused him blindness. He went to New York City for a while to seek treatment, but nothing prevented the inevitable. During his stay in New York, my mother went with him. She stayed in a flat where William Sr.'s wife, Hattie, lived. William had died in the 1930s, and Hattie was now living in the Harlem area with her children. My mother said that living in New York was horrific. There she was a girl from the rural Merrifield area living in New York City. What made matters worse was Hattie was not fond of my mother, and she let her know it. Mom felt that Hattie disliked her because she was darker-skinned than Hattie and her children. Whatever the case, Mother was there for more than a year. Yet one good thing prevailed: Hattie knew everyone in the black market and could get silk stockings, cigarettes and other liberties that were not provided during the war.

Hattie was also a good equestrian and gave riding lessons to the rich White children in and around New York. Hattie was not poor and lived a good life in New York.

Above: Photo of Guy V. Collins (*standing*) and Roscoe Collins (*playing guitar*) in the fellowship hall of the new church. *Courtesy of Robert "Bobbi" Whitmore.*

Left: Photo of Myra Collins-Lee, Helen Collins-Marshal and Birdie Terry, May 15, 1949. *Courtesy of author.*

Returning home to the Pines, Uncle Roscoe indeed lost his sight. But he still played the guitar and did construction work. Roscoe built his home and assisted Guy in building his. As a matter of fact, when Columbia Baptist in Falls Church needed a new roof, Uncle Roscoe was on the work team. Roscoe never let his blindness get in the way of living his life. Obstacles were merely an annoyance that could be sidestepped, and he did just that. Uncle Roscoe married Edith Turner and raised two children from another marriage: Evelyn and Constance.

Guy, the youngest of the siblings, was born on Christmas Day. He was also an exceptional individual and musician. At a young age, Grandma Lee taught him to play the piano. In his teenage years, he was the Senior Choir director, taking the place of Jennie Ransell. As a young adult, Guy took piano lessons in Washington, D.C., on the weekends, and he would take my mother and several of her siblings to travel with him to the city. He would give them twenty cents each for a movie ticket and popcorn, and they would go to Howard or the Lincoln theater to watch a picture show while Guy had his music lesson. In my mother's oral history, she stated that Uncle Guy, as he was known, was the first conductor of an interracial choir in Fairfax County. He also was the musical director for the Northern Virginia Baptist Association's choir. Guy married Edna Payne from Fairfax City, and they had four children: Rose Marie, Sylvia, Guy Jr. and William, all of whom were talented in music.

Helen, grandmother's sister, was married to William Beal Marshall; we called him Uncle Beal. They had eight children: Lloyd, Marshal, Garland, Lawrence, Helen and Ruby, as well as two who died in infancy. Myra married Avon Lee, whose grandfather was James E. Lee of Falls Church. The Lees were a prominent family within this area. My grandparents had eight children: Vernon, Eulala, Hazel, Myra, Leola, Dovella, Irene and Avonjeanette. Elburn Collins never married. He had a somewhat tragic life. When Elburn was young, he was accused of stealing a cow and was sentenced to ninety days in jail at the Fairfax Courthouse. Elburn's take on the accusation is that two White men asked him to butcher a cow they had purchased. Elburn was known for his abilities at butchering meat. Truth be told, the White men had stolen the cow, but Elburn was blamed. After his ninety days in jail, they say that he was never the same. He spent the rest of his life inebriated.

By the time I was born and visited the Pines, other people had taken up residence and built homes. Reverend Gray and his family and Mr. Tallow and his wife and daughter lived across the street from my grandmother.

Photo of the Collins grandchildren in the Pines. *Back row, from left to right*: Leonard Lee, Garland Marshall, James and Guy Collins Jr. *Courtesy of author*.

Photo of Fairfax County Historical Marker. Pictured are descendants of family members who established and lived at the Pines. *Courtesy of author*.

Ms. Thorton lived down the hill on Bannerwood Drive, along with Clarence Ransell. Sad to say, Utopia did not last long, as stated earlier. In 1965, the Fairfax County School Board decided to acquire the properties through eminent domain or condemnation. The board's reasoning for a total takeover of the Pines was to construct a desegregated high school to replace Luther Jackson "Colored" High.

Chapter 10

WILLIAMSTOWN

Born in April 1880, Seth Williams grew up in Fauquier County, Virginia. The 1900 census records show that Williams was living in that county with his mother. But in 1904, at the age of twenty-three, Williams married Marie Lee in Fauquier, Virginia. In 1904, Seth Williams and his wife moved to the Merrifield area to buy land. In 1919, Mr. Williams purchased fifteen acres of land from Ms. Effie W. Eskridge for the sum of $1,000. The land purchased was near the Pines and Merrifield and was located near Arlington Boulevard and Gallows Road. As with most Blacks in the area, Mr. Williams began farming. Like other farmers in Merrifield, he was a truck farmer who sold his produce at the K Street Market in Washington, D.C. Once a week, he and his wife, along with Jennie Ransell from the Pines, would travel to K Street to sell produce. Seth and his wife had children and quickly joined the First Baptist Church of Merrifield. Seth assisted in remodeling the old church, rang the bell on New Years and was chairman of the Trustee Board from the '40s into the '50s. He also was a devoted patron of the church. But more importantly, Seth was also a wise businessman.

By the 1930s, Seth Williams had begun to sell plots of land to displaced African Americans who had previously lived in East Arlington, Virginia. Prior to the establishing of East Arlington, African Americans during and after the Civil War lived in a section of Arlington called Freedman's Village. The village was property previously owned by Robert E. Lee, who abandoned his estate to fight on the side of the Confederacy. However, within twenty years of the war's end, these previously enslaved and their descendants were displaced. The removal from Freedman's Village forced the development of new African American communities such as Queen City and Hell's Bottom. The relocated settlements were now called East Arlington. But the relocation did not end there. With the building of the Pentagon in the 1930s, contractors realized that the space allocated for the building was not large enough. The federal government decided to evict more than 150 African American families from this part of Arlington, and the government took control of their land. Where could these disenfranchised people of color go? In the 1930s, Jim Crow was at its height.

With fifteen acres of land in the Providence District of Fairfax, and with Mr. Williams becoming older, he decided to sell property to Black folks from East Arlington, as his grandson William Smith, Jr. stated in his oral history, for the Civil Rights Archive of Northern Virginia. Mr. Smith said that he believed the Whitney family were the first family to buy land from his grandfather. These land sales led to the creation of Williamstown. By 1950, according to the census for the Providence District, Mr. Williams was surrounded by landowners: Levi Jones and his wife, Rosetta; Wilbur Jones; Chancy Johnson; Gertrude Whitney; Lafayette Nelson; and Willie Lambert and his wife, Bessie; along with Emanuel and Ester Calloway; the Newmans; the Wrights; and the Lansdowne.

When my grandparents moved to Williamstown, after being displaced from the Pines, a few residents in the area still had no indoor toilets or running water. However, most of the families still depended on wells for water, and as usual, in the Providence District, the Black neighborhoods had dirt or gravel roads. Most of the streets in African American neighborhoods were never paved, and never had gutters or sidewalks. When my grandparents purchased their land in Williamstown and built a two-story brick home, it had three bedrooms, two bathrooms, a basement with a fireplace and a laundry room with a washer and dryer. Their property sat next to the "White neighborhood," and as soon as you passed my grandparents' home, into the White section, you were driving on a black top road. The demarcation between Whites and Blacks was glaring.

Photo of Sammie McCormick, husband of Dovella Lee-McCormick, who lived on Javier Road. *Courtesy of author.*

However, Mr. Seth Williams saw no color. He sold land not only to Black individuals, but he also

Photos of homes in Williamstown, Fairfax, Virginia. *Courtesy of Avonjeannette Lee-Hill.*

Photos of homes on Javier Road, Fairfax, Virginia. The home pictured at bottom on the right is the home of Samuel and Dovella McCormick. *Courtesy of Avonjeannette Lee-Hill.*

sold to a gentleman from the Philippines, Mr. Fernando O. Javier, after whom Javier Road is named. Mr. Javier was born in the Philippines in 1898, the year the Spanish-American War started. He became a naturalized citizen and is listed on the 1930 and 1940 censuses as living with his wife, Anna, in Washington, D.C., and working at the Navy Yard. On the 1950 census, he is listed as living in the Providence District of Merrifield and serving in the navy as a chief steward petty officer. Javier purchased land from Seth Williams between 1940 and the 1950s. The property Javier purchased was behind what would later be known as the Luther Jackson "Negro" High School. During this time, this area became an offshoot Black community from Williamstown. My Aunt Dovella and Samuel McCormick owned land and a home on Javier Road. I loved that house and their yard, which had an outdoor barbecue pit. The extended families spent many summers roasting hot dogs, hamburgers and eating crabs at their home.

Even with Seth's business sense, Mr. Smith said that racism would not allow his grandfather into the bank at Fairfax Circle. When Mr. Williams had banking issues, he would go to a bank employee's home, where the man would assist him. Mr. Smith also said that his grandfather's house was burned to the ground by someone with grievances. Fortunately, this did not stop Seth, as he was an accomplished builder. He took his chicken coop,

Photo of Avon and Myra Lee's home in Williamstown. The home was built after land in the Pines was taken for eminent domain. *Courtesy of author.*

turned it into a home and then proceeded to build a better house made of brick. Seth's skill set for building was on display when he built the choir room, pastor study and choir gallery in the remodeling of the old church. He is also noted for replacing the steeple on the original church, as it was aging and becoming dangerous. Williams, after selling lots to other Black folks, even went so far as to assist landowners with building their homes. Seth Williams died on June 26, 1962. Dr. Harold Johnson, the only Black physician in the Merrifield area, signed the death certificate, and Mr. James Chinn, a Black undertaker, provided the funeral services.

As the 1970s and '80s rolled around, many homes were showing their age. The streets were still not paved, and there were still no sidewalks or streetlights in the Williamstown neighborhood. With desegregation and red lines being lifted in some parts of Fairfax County, many Black folks in Williamstown saw an opportunity to sell their land and purchase homes in neighborhoods with modern amenities. Developers were eager to scoop up their property, as its proximity to the nation's capital made the land purchases ideal. All but my grandparents sold and moved away, but Myra and Avon Lee were still living in their home when they passed away in the 1980s. When their children decided to sell the property, it was the last home sold in Williamstown. That brick house my grandparents built in 1965 is still there and is the last remaining remnant of Seth Williams's dream of a town for Blacks in Merrifield.

Chapter 11

James E. Lee

James E. Lee, the grandfather of my grandfather Avon Lee, was born in Fauquier County, Virginia, in the year 1842. This is relevant because James Lee was an early landowner in the Falls Church area after the Civil War, and later his grandson Avon married my grandmother, Myra Collins. Avon and Myra lived in the Pines on Myra's inherited property until the land was taken through eminent domain by Fairfax County in a geopolitical move that seemed to focus on Black communities.

My great-great-grandfather was never enslaved. James E. Lee and his brother Charles were born free. Being born free meant that at the time of someone's birth, their mother had to be free—either by birth or through manumission. The status of an individual as free or enslaved depends on their mother's freedom. James and Charles's mother was Betsy Lee, who was born-free in 1823. Betsy was free because her mother, Lucy Lee, was also born free in 1800. Lucy Lee, in turn, was born free because her mother was either born free or granted manumission. Considering the age Lucy's mother could have been at the time Lucy was conceived—and given that my DNA matches with the White Lee and Carter family—it is likely that she falls within the timeframe of Robert Carter III's gift of deed, which manumitted more than four hundred enslaved men, women and children.

By 1840, Lucy Lee, James's grandmother, was living in Leeds, Fauquier County, Virginia. Lucy's children, including her daughter Betsy, as well as Betsy's children James and Charles, registered as free people of color at the Fauquier County Courthouse.[155] As mandated by law, Lucy, her children and

James E. Lee, born free in 1843 and grandfather of Avon Lee. *Courtesy of author.*

her grandchildren were required to register as "Free Negroes" and obtain their "Free Negro papers." These papers needed to be renewed every three years at the courthouse in the county where they resided. On the same day in September 1842, Lucy, Betsy and her children James and Charles all registered as born-free in accordance with Virginia law. They were recorded in the Free Negro Registry in Fauquier County.[156] "The Act…to restrain the practice of negroes going at large" was passed on December 10, 1793, requiring that "[e]very Free Negroe and Mulatto, who resides in, or employed to labour within the limits of any city, borough or town, shall be registered and numbered in a book kept by the Town Clerk, which shall specify age, name, color, status, and by whom and in what court they were emancipated."[157] The free papers functioned like identification cards, certifying that a person of color was free either by birth or through manumission. Although registration was mandatory, it appears that the Lee family only registered once in Fauquier County.

Almost two decades later, in the 1860 census, Lucy Lee is listed as having property worth $100 and personal valuables estimated at $50.[158] It is believed that Lucy had entered into an agreement with Andrew Chunn, a wealthy landowner and enslaver living near her, to purchase land. But the agreement of purchase was never legally binding, and after the war she lost all rights to her land. This is supported by the fact that James and Charles filed a claim for a deed to the property, but the request was not approved.[159] As the threat of the Civil War loomed on the horizon, James and Charles were not living with their grandmother. Instead, they were on a list identifying where all "Free Negroes" were residing in the Fauquier County. James and Charles were listed as laborers on Andrew Chunn's plantation.

At the beginning of the war, when Southern states seceded from the Union, the Confederate government enacted the Public Service Act. This act, as described by the Library of Virginia, noted the following:

> *In July 1861, the state convention that had approved secession passed an ordinance "to provide for the enrollment and employment of free Negroes*

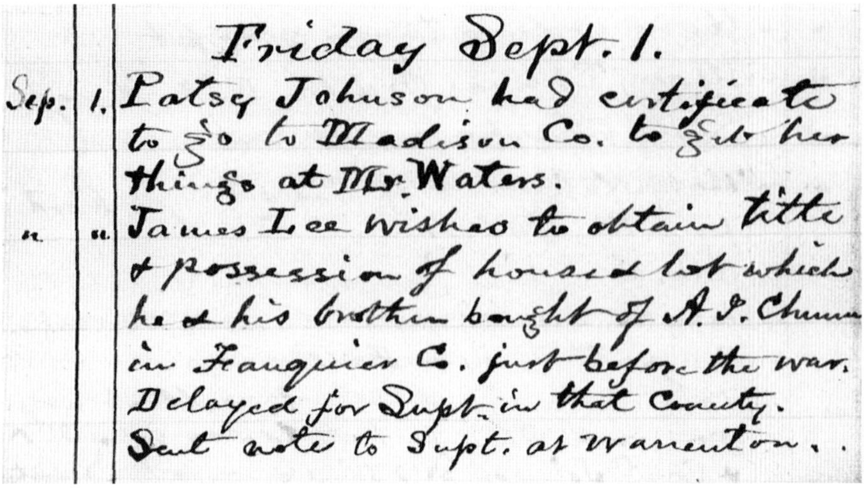

Friday Sept. 1.

Sep. 1. Patsy Johnson had certificate to go to Madison Co. to get her things at Mr. Waters.

" " James Lee wishes to obtain title & possession of house & lot which he & his brother bought of A. J. Chunn in Fauquier Co. just before the war. Delayed for Supt. in that County. Sent note to Supt. at Warrenton. .

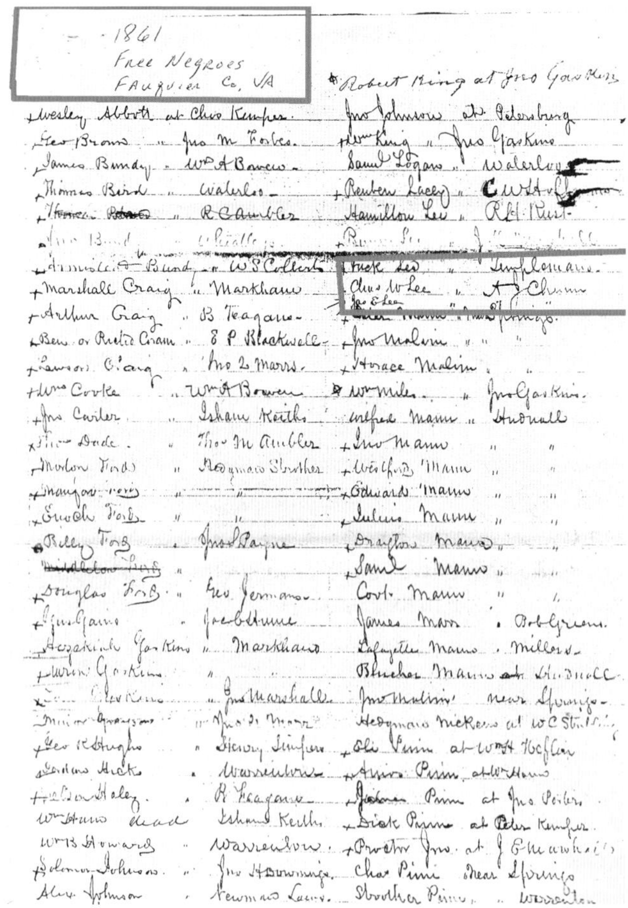

1861
Free Negroes
Fauquier Co, VA

Chas W Lee " A J Chunn

Above: Written request by James Lee to take possession of the house and lot that he and his brother had bought from A.J. Chunn. *Courtesy of Wayne Hubbard.*

Left: "Free Negroes," Fauquier County, Virginia, 1861. Charles and James Lee are listed as living on A.J. Chunn's farm. *Courtesy of Ellie Hill.*

Opposite: Historical marker in Centreville, Virginia, of the bunker site that James E. Lee may have helped dig for the Confederate army in 1861, probably by force. *Courtesy of author.*

> *in the public service." This ordinance was amended and re-enacted by the General Assembly in February 1862. The legislation authorized local courts to enroll for "public use" all able-bodied male free African Americans between the ages of eighteen and fifty. They would not serve more than 180 days and would be fairly compensated for their services.*
>
> *When a commanding officer of the Confederate Army had need of the services of free African Americans, a local board would select from the list of free African Americans "such number of laborers as in their judgment may be proper and expedient." The local sheriff would notify the free African Americans of their selection and the location where they were to report for their "public service." If a free African American did not report for duty, he would be subject to the same penalties as a white man drafted into the militia who failed to report.*[160]

On October 13, 1861, this act from the Confederacy affected my great-great-grandfather James. His name was listed on a letter sent to Jno. G. Beckham on behalf of General Johnston to obtain four to five hundred "free Negro" men to be sent to Centreville, Virginia, and dig entrenchments for the Confederate army's winter encampment.[161] It is not known if James was paid for his labor; however, it is known that if he didn't go, he could suffer some sort of punishment to include possible lynching. The choice was not his to make.

The line in the photo indicates the outline of the entrenchments that James E. Lee may have helped dig. *Courtesy of author.*

What is known is that Charles Lee joined the Tenth United States Colored Troop, Company G, and after the war both James and Charles came to Falls Church, Virginia. In a letter James dictated in 1919, he stated that he and Charles, like other Freedmen in the area, purchased land from another retired Union officer, Colonel John S. Crocker. Crocker and his brother William were land speculators. The Crockers created wealth by buying property and reselling it to Freedmen in the Falls Church area. James and his brother purchased eight acres of land for $400 on December 27, 1866.[162] The Southgate subdivision, where the Lees purchased property, was established by a White land speculator named M.E. Church. It was a collection of narrow lots paralleling two streets, Liberty and Douglas. Its border ran from Hillwood Avenue, near the home of Harriett Brice, to what is considered Arlington Boulevard today.[163] This community is where James and Charles Lee purchased their property from John Crocker in 1866. It is also the home of Second Baptist Church; Southgate is still a predominantly Black community.[164] By August 1869, the Lee brothers had a clear title to the property, and with land acquired, both brothers began their new lives as farmers, living off their own labor. Like many of the Freedmen landowners, both James and Charles were truck farmers, growing and selling produce to markets in Washington, D.C. Oral history also states that James had beautiful horses and a carriage, and he rented out his horses and rig to people for special occasions.[165] An early tax assessment for James revealed that he did own a carriage, horses, a clock and a sewing machine. Additionally, James's home was apparently immaculate, as he would win a prize every year for the best gardens in Falls Church.[166]

In May 1871, James Lee was listed on the deed as a trustee for the purchasing of two acres of land for the church, sold to him by a White citizen named George Pulver for $150.[167] He was also listed as a trustee in two land purchases to establish the Second Baptist Church. Purchases were made on July 7, 1871, for half an acre for $30 from Stephen Bowman, another Freedman and his wife, and again on July 7, 1871, for another half an acre, purchased for $30 from George and Harriett Brice. In 1872, the Second Baptist Church of Falls Church was constructed, and James E. Lee was listed as one of the first trustees. Other Blacks listed on the church's land deeds were Andrew Tillman, an early Freedman landowner, and Eli Blackwell. Charles, on the other hand, was instrumental with the opening of the Galloway Methodist Church, also in Falls Church, Virginia. It is interesting to note that many of the founding parishioners within First Baptist of Merrifield—such as the Lees, Collins's, Tinners, Hyson's, Fishes, Turners, Burkes, Terrys and Gaskins—were also relatives of the founders of the Second Baptist Church and Galloway Methodist Church in Falls Church.

James and his brother Charles were the fourth generation of Freedmen born into this family. Uneducated due to the laws enacted in Virginia before the war and having limited resources, these Freedmen, during Reconstruction, bought land and helped establish a thriving Black community in Falls Church, Virginia. After James Lee's death in 1923, Russell Lee, James's son, donated land he inherited from his father for the "Colored School," which was named the James Lee Elementary School. It is now known as the James E. Lee Community Center.

An interesting side note is that in 1888, James Lee was unable to attend his daughter Betsy's wedding, so he wrote a note stating that he and his wife were unable to attend the wedding but, "willing for Mr. Arthur Woody to have their Bessie Lee."[168] To this day, relatives of the Lees still live in the area, and they all know the secret. It has been spoken in hushed corners of rooms and passed down for decades by their ancestors: they believe that James and Charles Lee were the sons of General Robert E. Lee. Both

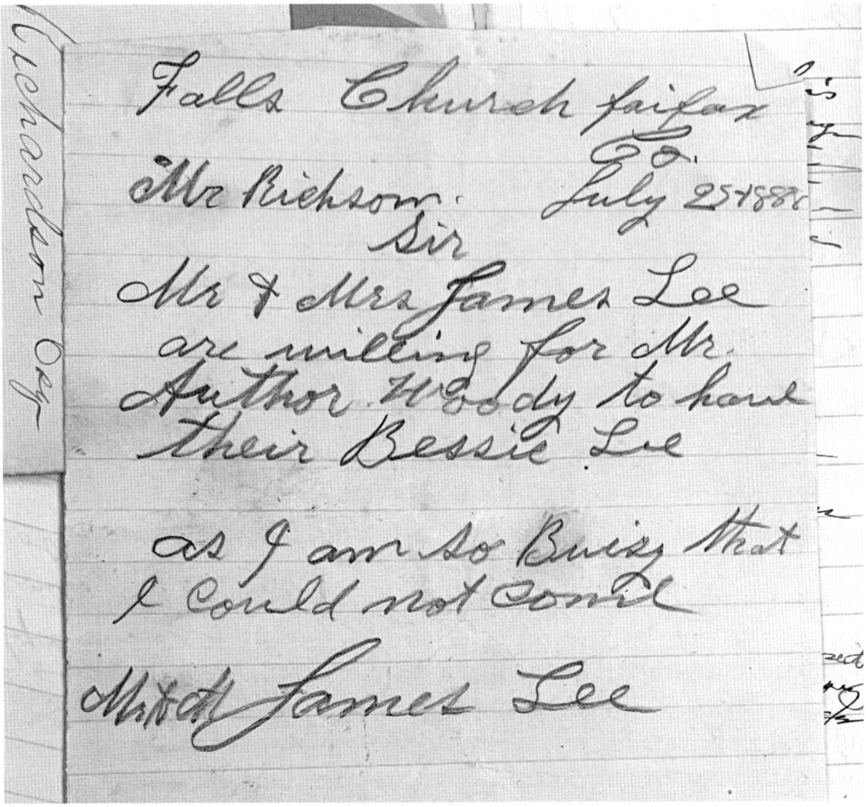

Falls Church fairfax Co.
Mr Richson July 25 1888
Sir
Mr & Mrs James Lee
are willing for Mr.
Author Woody to have
their Bessie Lee

as I am so Buisy that
I could not come
Mr & M James Lee

Letter written by James Lee giving permission for his daughter Bessie Lee to marry Mr. Arthur Woody, July 25, 1888. *Courtesy of the Fairfax County Archives.*

James and Charles were the same ages as Robert E. Lee's White children. Robert had family members with property in Fauquier and Fairfax County. However, most importantly, DNA shows that James and Charles are related to the White Lees, possibly Robert E. Lee, as their ancestors' oral histories have stated.

Chapter 12

The Northern Virginia Baptist Association

In 1977, President Jimmy Carter sent an official White House letter of acknowledgement to the Northern Virginia Baptist Association with congratulatory remarks for one hundred years of service, dedicated to benevolence within the community by creating a "strong and positive influence in a country where religious liberty is a way of life."[169]Acknowledging religious liberty, the question must be asked as to why this organization was necessary in 1877?

How and why did it provide affirmative influence in the Black community of Northern Virginia? Was this association conceived within the communities as a pathway toward leadership where disenfranchisement for people of color was becoming the status quo? Was it organized to bind together a strong coalition for socioeconomic stability?

The Northern Virginia Baptist Association (NVBA) was established to complement the Black churches and address some of the communities' social concerns. This included education, property, ownership and control over their labor. Freedmen also wanted the ability to practice religion in the matter of their choosing most of all, and the ability to circumvent the financial tethering associated with White farmers through sharecropping or tenant farming. As stated previously, many felt the equalizing factor for autonomy within Northern Virginia was landownership, education and religious sovereignty. All in all, the economic stability of landownership facilitated church building and academic opportunities to offset disenfranchisement and to make available a better way of life for their families.

Likewise, to extend the radius of solidarity within the local congregations, religious leaders began to build church associations, such as the one that originated in 1877 in Northern Virginia. These Black religious and civic societies offered welfare assistance, contributed to missionary work, facilitated the construction of schools and churches and provided necessities for widows, orphans, retired ministers and students. Along those same lines, there were families who needed assistance in burying their dead or help with financial issues from illness or loss of a spouse. Additionally, hardships could be brought about by legal problems through the inequality of justice. Furthermore, missionary work to aid orphans, widows and the elderly was always in the forefront. Without the benefit of the Black community, little aid could be expected from the county, which was controlled by the White citizenry. Groups such as the Northern Virginia Baptist Association provided an additional layer of religious stability to offset inequalities in schooling and the judicial arena, as well as caring for those less fortunate and the disenfranchised.

Beginnings of the Religion in Northern Virginia

The indoctrination of a White religious creed forced many of the enslaved to seek an "invisible institution." They were forced to worship in secret, invisible to the slave owner's eyes. They worshiped within the darkness of the woods, hollows, thickets, their slave cabins or bush harbors.[170] Usually led by a Black exhorter, these secret meetings allowed the enslaved to sing, dance and worship the God they felt would eventually provide them with freedom, much like he did with the Israelites and Moses. As Albert J. Raboteau maintained in his book *Canaan Land: A Religious History of African Americans*, "the desire for 'real preaching'"—that is, sermons free of proslavery propaganda—"pushed the slaves to hold their own religious gatherings."[171] Research has also shown that Freedmen, just like those in Mills-Crossroads who were once required to suffer the religious corseting of White Christian dogma, used their newfound freedom to worship openly. They also expanded their religious reach by establishing such religious institutions as the Northern Virginia Baptist Association. This type of spiritual unity among numerous church affiliates provided an additional layer of protection against racism. So it is not surprising that the individual religious institutions in Northern Virginia joined together as a bulwark against injustice.

Furthermore, for many African American men, it afforded leadership opportunities within a sphere of autonomy contrasting the paternalistic environment of enslavement. Freedmen expressed their dissatisfaction with the lack of respect and blatant discrimination from White religious institutions by detaching from White churches and forming their own spiritual institutions. In Northern Virginia, they quickly understood that churches were central to their social, economic and educational independence. They also realized the power of unity and the ability to achieve equality through numbers.

Also, many in the local congregations were already landowners even before the NVBA was formally established. In Fairfax County land acquisition activity pursued by Blacks between the 1870s and the early 1900s is evident. It is also not surprising that the establishment of the Northern Virginia Baptist Association came in 1877, with early churches founded in the area, such as Mount Pleasant in 1868 and Second Baptist of Falls Church, along with First Baptist Church of Merrifield established in the early 1870s.

Records seem to indicate, directly after the Civil War, there had not been a distinction between the African American Baptist and Methodist denominations, and Reverend Read, a White minister in Falls Church encouraged Blacks to establish their own seats of worship.[172] The Falls Church Freedmen, of which James and Charles Lee were a part, grouped together and divided into factions, creating two churches: Galloway Methodist and Second Baptist.[173] The rationale behind the division is not documented, so the reason behind the separation may never be known. However, insight comes from George Thomas, a Falls Church Freedmen and a former slave of Cook Fitzhugh. In Thomas's narrative, written in 1928, he declares the divide may have been caused by Blacks who came into Falls Church after the war. He maintained that in 1865, Baptist prayer leaders Thomas Green and Bill Stuart came into the town after service in the army and began to hold prayer meetings along with Methodist prayer leaders George Rumbles and Nathan Rumbles.[174] Blacks already living in Falls Church may have befriended either the Baptist or the Methodist prayer leaders, thereby causing a separation in worship. Divisions of worship were also made between family members.[175] James Lee became a trustee of Second Baptist, while his brother and neighbor became a member and trustee of Galloway Methodist.[176] Members of First Baptist of Merrifield, who had been worshiping at Second Baptist started worshiping in a log cabin on Graham Road in Falls Church and later in Mills-Crossroads. White ministers, such as Reverend Hiram Read, were also instrumental in providing marriage ceremonies denied to Blacks while enslaved. In 1867, Read oversaw the nuptials for James Lee's mother, Betsy, who married James Strothers in 1868.

Although former slaves in Falls Church, and the Mills-Crossroads area saw themselves as Freedmen, many still suffered from the lack of independence and full citizenship outlined in the Fourteenth and Fifteenth Amendments to the Constitution. Sadly, by 1896, the Supreme Court ruling in the case *Plessy v. Ferguson* had legalized the "separate but equal" framework, which altered the course of history and solidified Jim Crow laws, making the need for a unified Northern Virginia Baptist Association even more prevalent. It was this court ruling to allow unequal standards for school facilities, public accommodations and transportation that became the steppingstone toward disenfranchisement of African Americans in Northern Virginia and Fairfax County. As the turn of the century approached, the White, politically powerful elites made changes to the Virginia Constitution, such as eliminating the voting rights of Black males, thereby strengthening the state and local jurisdictions with regards to the disenfranchisement for people of color.

Although, by 1877, African Americans in Fairfax were becoming landowners, church patrons and educational participants, they still felt the need for a centrally focused organization to provide support to their local churches regarding the problems of marginalization, morality and temperance during the nadir era of African American history. The year 1877 saw the beginning of the organizational meetings of the Northern Virginia Baptist Association, held within the walls of the First Baptist Church of Warrenton.[177] The designated church in Warrenton, had already been in existence since 1867 under the leadership of Reverend Waring. He and his charter members purchased property in 1867 on Lee Street in Warrenton for $400 to establish the church.[178] The one-hundred-year anniversary book claims that the founders were all former slaves still living within the Warrenton area when the congregation was formed. Historiography has shown that the organizing of religious societies directly after emancipation was not uncommon, and this area was no different.

After its establishment, the NVBA assisted small churches in spreading throughout the region, grouping together and forming a network of communication. This network, listed in the 1891 minutes, facilitated assistance with issues pertaining to morality, temperance, education, injustices and Christianity.[179] Early minute books show that the charter churches were within the borders of Fairfax, Prince William, Loudoun, Fauquier, Stafford, Page,

Warren, Greene, Rappahannock, Culpeper, Orange and Madison Counties, as well as a few in certain parts of West Virginia.[180]

Warrenton Baptist was a logical facility to oversee the first organization meeting of the association, as it was one of the earliest Black churches established in the area and it claimed more members than any other church in the region.[181] Furthermore, Blacks living near the borders of Prince William and Warrenton County were close to one another and were busy organizing a vocational school for Black youth. This school, Manassas Industrial School for Colored Youth, was the brainchild of Miss Jennie Dean, who had been enslaved on the Cushing Plantation near the present-day Manassas Battlefield.[182] Dean is listed in 1891 for the NVBA's convention held at Pleasant Grove, in Orange County, as a leader for the Sunday School Union and the Moral and Temperance Committee. Because Dean was involved in organizing a secondary school, and because First Baptist of Warrenton had the largest membership of any church, this may be the reason for the first conferences to be held outside Fairfax County. Furthermore, the original moderator of the association was Reverend Marshall D. Williams, DD, the minister for First Baptist of Warrenton at the time.[183] Of the ministers who organized churches in Fairfax, none had an educational background or a Doctor of Divinity degree, except for Reverend Williams.

In July 1889, a group of twenty-one churches met in Culpeper at the Antioch Baptist Church.[184] A resolution was drafted to organize an additional association in the region, as the breadth of churches within NVBA was large. The main reasons for the division involved mobility and transportation issues for such a large organization spreading from the borders of Washington, D.C., to West Virginia. This resolution was passed, and another group, the New Wayland Blue Ridge Association, was created and went on to serve the churches in and around the Culpeper area. However, the Northern Virginia Baptist Association continued to serve the churches within Fairfax, such as First Baptist Church of Merrifield and Second Baptist in Falls Church.[185]

An overview of responsibilities listed within the initial constitutional bylaws for NVBA notes that the "objects of this Association shall be for fraternal intercourse and mutual counsel: to promote the union of churches: to promote Christian and general education: to advance the cause of Christ by all means consistent with the Word of God."[186] Added goals within the Baptist Association was to assist the community churches in sustaining themselves financially and also creating new religious facilities in the area.[187] These associations, such as the NVBA, gave congregations and especially Black males an opportunity to gather together, voice their opinions on current topics and provide support for new churches, schools and missionaries.[188]

Examination of minutes from the fourteenth annual meeting in 1891 provides a valuable opportunity for comprehending African American agency within Northern Virginia. Few official minutes still exist, leaving a void for reconstructing the history of the organization, however with the existence of the 1891 minutes provides an overview of each member church's fiscal and Christian responsibilities. Member churches would list the number of converts for that year, along with the number of deaths and the amount of money given to the convention for home and foreign missionaries. Along those same lines, the amount of money given for school and Christian education was enumerated. These amounts varied from twenty-five cents to two dollars. Also identified were the officers: a moderator, first and second vice-moderators, corresponding secretary and an association clerk. As mentioned earlier, the first moderator for the association was Reverend Marshall D. Williams of Manassas, Virginia. Williams maintained the position until his health failed in 1923. In 1926, Reverend George W. Powell, DD, of Second Baptist Church in Falls Church was elected as moderator and maintained that position until he passed in 1933. In 1954, another minister of Second Baptist Church, Reverend Wallace Earl Costner of Falls Church, Virginia, became moderator. Reverend Costner was also an advocate for the creation of an African American high school in Fairfax County.

In an oral history interview obtained in April 2014, Reverend Kenny Smith, DD, of First Baptist Church in Vienna maintains the reason for the association was community cohesiveness. As a former moderator of the association, Reverend Smith stated, "The association was formed so Blacks could congregate together a couple of days in August and continue communication, along with solidifying community."[189] In the early part of the association's history, these actions were vital when dealing with disenfranchisement and Jim Crow. In the years of the civil rights movement, Reverend Smith stated the NAACP worked closely with the NVBA in protesting segregation. Reverend Smith during this period was also the president of the Fairfax County NAACP.

The churches would gather in the third week of August, and they brought with them leadership skills, pride and a desire for autonomy for their own churches and communities. Leadership roles and committee memberships were divided among those delegates sent to the NVBA by the member churches. Usually, the meetings were divided into three parts. The morning session lasted from 9:00 a.m. to 1:00 p.m. The afternoon session ran between 3:00 p.m. and 6:00 p.m. The evening session started at 8:00 p.m. and had no set end time. The morning sessions were mandated to begin with a sermon, and the following session was led by prayer. Each session gave reports pertaining to committee issues of church growth, benevolent responsibilities, educational scholarships to seminaries and missionary work. Missionary work was central to the NVBA. In one session of the 1891 meeting, a resolution was passed to thank the railroad company for reducing rate fares for riders coming into Orange County for the convention.[190]

To help facilitate a greater ability to provide both local and state missions, the Women's Auxiliary was added to the main body in 1914. Mrs. Maria H. Lucas became its first president.[191] In 1939, President Dora Lucas recommended in her address to the convention to establish an "old folks' home" for aging ministers in keeping with the mission statement of the association to care for the widows, orphans and the clergy. The motion for a home was met with overwhelming enthusiasm. The women raised enough money to purchase a parcel of land located in Odrick's Corner (McLean), Virginia, for $2,300. However, because of segregated accommodation, the focus changed.

In 1951, the women sold their property in Odrick's Corner and purchased 23.9 acres of property from Mr. and Mrs. Thomas Lambert (who had become unable to work their farm) on Glenkirk Road in Gainesville Virginia.

The website for the NVBA notes:

> *The establishment of the Baptist Center was initiated when construction began on 2 barracks, a dining room and a kitchen in 1957. A swimming pool was later constructed and dedicated on June 25, 1960. The pavilion was constructed and dedicated with the laying of its corner stone on May 30, 1966. It was named the ROSS-PENN Memorial Building in honor of Rev. Samuel B. Ross who served as Moderator of the Association, 1945 to 1954 and Ms. Adeline Penn who served as president of the Women Auxiliary 1945 to 1950. Both individuals had a part in the inception of the Center and work untiringly to this cause up until their death. Other improvements at the center include the expansion of the dining facility and more recently, the construction of an educational wing onto the pavilion.*[192]

For many years, the center ran summer camps for youth by dedicated individuals such as Mrs. Pauline Gray, whose husband had been the Pastor of Second Baptist Church in Clifton. There are too many others who dedicated their time and effort to the camps to mention. Several individuals from the Merrifield area contributed significantly. Reverend Veron Pettus and his wife, Sue, provided arts and crafts along with physical education to the youth. Additionally, Ms. Shirley Terry of Merrifield assisted Ms. Gray each year.

This facility—created by African Americans through faith, family, friendship and community—allowed Blacks to vent their frustration with marginalization, provided leadership roles within their segregated communities and instilled in the youth the way toward a better tomorrow.

The NVBA was surely needed, as the subjugation of Blacks and the groundwork for segregation can be looked on as byproducts of the short-lived Reconstruction era. On June 12, 1901, one hundred delegates convened in Richmond to begin the dialogue for a new state constitution. As African Americans had little to no voice within this process, their equality, won through Constitutional amendments, was slipping away in the Old Dominion. This debate lasted for nearly a year and ended on April 4, 1902, with a new constitution based on a platform that featured the complete disenfranchisement of Blacks. John Goode, a conservative Democrat, stated, "Voting rights, in particular those enjoyed by African Americans, would be a subject of transcendent interest and importance to the convention....The right of suffrage is not a natural right." He continued, "It is a social right and must necessarily be regulated by society. Virginia, within her borders, can regulate it according to her own sovereign will and pleasure, provided she does not violate the Constitution of the United States." Using the 1902 constitution as a starting point, it is clear that Virginia wanted to regulate social order based on the ideology of White supremacist dogma. It is this very action that created the need for the Northern Virginia Baptist Association as a way to galvanize Black communities to raise up as a collective voice against racism and segregation.[193]

As previously mentioned, only a few minutes remain in the early sessions of the NVBA. Current members of the association have shared oral histories that highlight the importance of its mission. Many, including Avonjeannette Lee-Hill and Viola Richardson, emphasize the value of churches coming together cooperatively to combat segregation and inequality. Avonjeannette stated, "My ancestors who helped create First Baptist of Merrifield were also involved with the association and the Baptist Center."[194] She continued, "It was important to them because it gave them significance, self-esteem and a way to organize when things were not going well racially."[195] Avonjeannette remembered how when someone needed assistance financially or was in trouble with the law, often their only recourse was the church or the NVBA.

The Northern Virginia Baptist Association is still a viable thread woven into the fabric of Fairfax Counties Black religious organizations. It has more than 120 member churches active within the Northern Virginia area. The land in Gainesville is still owned by the association and is valued at $1 million per acre. Today, an annual meeting is held on the grounds in the third week in August. The work of missions and church building continues. Sadly, since the passing of Pauline Terry Gray, the coordinator of the youth summer camps, the camps have been discontinued, and even though the Black communities in Merrifield, the Pines and Williamstown no longer exist, the association still plays a pivotal role in aiding churches, families and individuals with judicial and financial problems. NVBA continues to work in collaboration with the NAACP and other civic organizations on any problems that may arise.

CHAPTER 13

WHY ARE THEY ALL GONE?

The Pines was lost due to what is believed to be racially motivated acts on the part of the Fairfax County School Board. Many landowners felt that the board deliberately acquired the property of Black landowners in the Pines as retaliation against desegregation of the school system. At least, that is what my grandmother Myra always thought. To give only sixty days to vacate property a family has owned for decades. To never build a school, desecrate a cemetery and pour excess dirt onto the land, all the while creating a recreational space and gardens for people who know nothing of the struggles Blacks endure to purchase and maintain the property the county took, is outrageous.

In a news article dated April 14, 2000, in the *Washington Post*, it was revealed that on February 8, 1965, the official minutes of the school board referred to the Collins property as "colored property."[196] Another county memo dated March 5 of the same year noted that the site had five homes, "none of which had a very high value." The Collins siblings, who owned land in the Pines, were mortgage-free, having inherited the property from their father, William Collins Jr. For these siblings, the land held more value than money, it was a part of their identity and served as a reminder of who they were as hardworking people of color.

The Collins family were given a choice: take a buy-out or we will condemn your property. In the end, the property was taken, with Guy Collins receiving $26,000, Roscoe Collins $11,000, Helen Marshall and Elburn Collins together receiving $14,500.[197] The school board also purchased 2.5 acres of

Left: The Pines in 1966. In front of Myra Collin-Lee's home is Don Bonds, sitting on the car hood. Denise Bonds is in the middle, and Carol Bonds is holding the shovel. *Courtesy of author.*

Below: Photo of Myra Collins-Lee in front of her brother Roscoe's home in the Pines. Myra's farm is in the background. *Courtesy of author.*

land owned jointly by the family for $7,000. None of the payouts from the school board were enough for the Collins siblings to purchase land and build new homes. This meant that they had to take out mortgages. Finding land to settle on was also difficult, as many places were segregated and red-lined.

My grandmother and grandfather purchased property from Seth Williams and built a home in Williamstown. In the late '70s, my grandmother was interviewed by an NBC reporter. She told them, "That community, they just wiped it out. Nothing else will feel like home."

To make matters worse, the property was vacant for decades. The first use of the property was to allow Mobil Oil Company to dump dirt onto the land from the complex it built in Merrifield. In the same article, by the Washington Post Mr. Tom Brady, assistant superintendent for facilities services, stated, "The school system has 16 other sites like Pine Ridge, acquired years ago for schools that ultimately were never built. But returning the land to its previous owners wouldn't be prudent." He went on to say, "We keep the land because we may need it. It makes, I think, remarkably sound business sense to keep it….What goes up in value? Land." Supervisor Penelope A. Gross, whose Mason District includes Pine Ridge, said that the site was acquired through legal means for public use. "Whether it became a school or is now used as

Myra Collins-Lee's home in the Pines in 1958, before it was remodeled. The remodeled home was taken through eminent domain by Fairfax County. *Courtesy of author.*

a park, that is still public space." In 2000, the Fairfax County School Board transferred the ownership of my ancestors' property to the Fairfax County Park Authority. The park authority created soccer fields and continued the practice of allowing locals to create garden plots.[198]

Merrifield was sold because of pressure from Fairfax County, citing sanitation ordinances and blight regulations. Many of the people in Merrifield did not have running water or indoor plumbing. Of course, when the county demanded they get upgrades for indoor plumbing, these Black families did not have the money to do so. If they then went to a bank to try for a loan, they were turned down. Along came people who are willing to purchase the land, and the neighborhood is no more. The Liberty Lodge is gone. The Odd Fellows Hall is gone. Vincent Store is no more. The Black schoolhouses have been torn down. What is left is Ransell Road, named after Deacon Freddie Ransell. The old church has been demolished, but the new church and the handmade cabinets Freddie built for the kitchen are still standing. Luther Jackson is still a proud brick place of learning for desegregated education. The rest is gone. They are found only in the collected memory of those who lived, were educated and worshipped in these spaces.

Ernestine Moss-Baker sledding at the farm in the Pines. *Courtesy of author.*

Photo of homes on Porter Road in 1950s. On the left is the Merrifield Colored School, and to the right is Mr. Brickhouse's home. Brown's delivery truck is in the driveway at Eulala Lee-Ransell's home. *Courtesy of author.*

By the 1980s, Williamstown was in a position where both the Pines and Merrifield were no longer the vibrant, close-knit community it had once been. Without the stability of Black neighbors and neighborhoods and the pressure from land developers to purchase property, Black families began selling their homes, and Williamstown became a distant memory—all except for my grandmother Myra and her husband, Avon. They held on to the property until they both were deceased, and their children sold the land to a realtor. The home my grandparents built on that dusty, dirt road called Williams Drive is still standing. It has been remodeled by the current owners, but it is the last remnant of Williamstown. Although it has been remodeled, it still stands on the original footprint where the brick foundation was laid. I look at the loss of Williamstown as I do the happenings in Prince William County, where developers are scarring the landscape with data centers in the name of progress, and all the while paying landowners unbelievable amounts of money to sell out. I can't blame landowners for selling, but what is left after they sell is a vacancy of history, wrapped in the veil of progress, that decades later will be forgotten.

CONCLUSION

In 1977, when President Jimmy Carter provided the congratulatory message to the Northern Virginia Baptist Association, he did so to legitimize the work the NVBA had done for the Black communities it served. This book has shown the roles of the Black pioneers, former slaves and freed persons of color in Fairfax County who desired to acquire land; create homes, churches, businesses and schools; and organize a Baptist association within Northern Virginia. James Lee expressed this in his biographical letter, archived at Second Baptist Church in the 1920s.[199] In Lee's mind, landownership made him a true citizen.[200] It is interesting to note that many of the ancestors within Mills-Crossroads/Merrifield, the Pines, Williamstown and Falls Church are still living within thirty miles of their original families' homesteads. I am one of those family members. Ancestors before me knew that landownership could lead to an easier road in establishing schools, churches and benevolent organizations such as the Odd Fellows Hall and the Liberty Lodge. It was made easier because much of the land for the schools was donated by Freedmen, along with the property for community churches. Yet as Reconstruction crumbled, the church and associations became even more significant. The association in Northern Virginia assisted Black individuals in unifying their efforts against marginalization and Jim Crow.

The association played a crucial role in providing educational resources, religious instruction, civic awareness and leadership opportunities for African Americans prior to emancipation. The minutes from the 1891

NVBA conference clearly detail how the association supported education, morality, temperance and Christian values. Furthermore, these minutes offer an in-depth examination of the emergence of leadership and autonomy that was otherwise restricted within the secular society of White Northern Virginia.

This book has outlined the importance of landownership, Black religion and churches within Mills-Crossroads, Merrifield, the Pines and Williamstown. The areas around Mills-Crossroads/Merrifield are still considered the Upper South, yet they have morphed into a diverse and unique organism due in part to the area's proximity to the nation's capital, Maryland and other border states. Additionally, Northern Virginia, after the war, started to manifest it's self toward the direction of a northern society based on modernization and industrialization. Along those same lines, a diversified agricultural community afforded farmers limited autonomy and means to financially support their families and communities. Moreover, the importance of northern land speculators—such as General Crocker, Robert Porter, O.M. Hines and other Whites who sold land to Freedmen—cannot be overlooked. These Whites provided an avenue of landownership for Blacks after emancipation.

Emphasis has been placed on the significance of landownership, Black religion and churches in the areas of Mills-Crossroads/Merrifield, the Pines and Williamstown. Although their communities were part of the South, they evolved into diverse and unique spaces.

Yet White supremacy still lived within the county's borders. As more Black families moved away from the area's urban centers and into the county to purchase cheap farmland, some Whites felt threatened. Many correlated this influx to the modern transportation available to and from the county. These concerns were outlined in an article published in 1904 by the *Fairfax Herald*: "The trolley had brought a large number of lawless characters to the county [including] some of the Negroes employed on the new electric railroad.…When attempted…we would advise our people to pump lead into the rowdies until they become fit subjects for a junk shop." Furthermore, a popularized incident was reported in the *Herald* when a Black woman, Barbara Pope, living in Washington and traveling to Falls Church, refused to move to the back of the trolley when the train arrived in Fairfax. She was arrested for breaking Jim Crow laws and incarcerated for twenty-four hours, and when Pope brought a suit against the train company, she was "awarded one cent in damages."[201] Incidents such as these strengthened unity within the Black communities.

Despite the passage of decades and the loss of generations, the ideals of freedom, education, religious expression and landownership remained active among the African Americans of Northern Virginia and their descendants. Reconstruction was a period filled with uncertainty and change. However, it was the resilience and determination of the Freedmen that enabled them to become landowners. Through landownership, they created new social and religious opportunities. The resilience, frugality and optimism of these individuals—such as Joshua Ball, Joshua Pearson, William Collins Jr. and Seth Williams—empowered them to navigate the uncharted seas of landownership, education, freedom and financial stability in areas such as Mills-Crossroads, the Pines and Williamstown.

This book is a labor of love. It was written to provide a road map of the struggles and successes of my ancestors and those who lived in these spaces and the organizations they created. Many came from enslavement and bore the brunt of establishing themselves and their families from nothing more than pure desire and determination. Others, who were never considered enslaved but who were still deprived of their civil rights, walked in the same shoes as those newly freed. These persons of color and their families saw an opportunity to build communities, and they did.

By the time civil rights came to Northern Virginia, many Black communities were lost. Merrifield was lost to elected officials who used sanitation rules and blight ordinances to force Blacks to sell their land. The Pines was taken by eminent domain for a high school that was never built, and Williamstown's landowners felt the pinch of progress and willingly sold their property to businesses. Residents of Northern Virginia, both Black and White, often have no recollection of the areas that are so vividly captured in my mind where Black communities thrived. Many believe that Merrifield has always been a bustling center of commerce. Most are shocked when they learn the truth of the area's origins. But Mills-Crossroads/Merrifield, the Pines and Williamstown were spaces of Blackness that must never be forgotten or be lost in Virginia's history.

I dedicate this book to my beloved mother, Eulala E. Lee-Ransell, who had only a seventh-grade education and who suffered great losses but never lost her smile. To my grandmother Myra Collins-Lee. I hope the tears you shed in the loss of your beloved Pines may be wiped away by the words I wrote and the memories I have collected. To Wayne Dobbins, thank you. Sheree, Jasmin, Charlie, Arianna, Charlotte and Finley—you are the breath I take each day and the reason for my living. I love you all to the moon and back. Acknowledgements must also go to Aunt Dolly—

Avonjeanette Lee-Hill—whose dedication to maintaining the history of these areas makes her the authentic griot of Northern Virginia. Without Aunt Dolly's wisdom and guidance, I would not have known where to start. A special thank-you goes to my cousin Joyce Gray-Bellamy, whose dedication to First Baptist Church of Merrifield (FBCM) history will make the ancestors proud.

NOTES

Preface

1. Dunn interview, 1971.

Chapter 1

2. Sweig, "Brief History of Fairfax County."
3. Shuman, *Mantua*.
4. Hardy, *Standin' On Faith*; Oberle, "Total Population of Fairfax County by Race."
5. Pargas, *Quarters and the Fields*.
6. Pargas, *Quarters and the Fields*.
7. Brawley, *Social History of the American Negro*.
8. Foner, *Reconstruction*.
9. Foner, *Reconstruction*.
10. Brundage, *Lynching in the New South*, 152.
11. Andrew Wolf, "Black Settlement in Fairfax County, Virginia during Reconstruction." Wolf's information comes from land deeds in Fairfax County and an oral history with William West. Oral histories with West are kept at the George Mason Archives in Fairfax, Virginia.
12. Wolf, "Black Settlement in Fairfax County, Virginia."

Chapter 2

13. Sweig, "Brief History of Fairfax County."
14. Sweig, "Brief History of Fairfax County."
15. Sweig, "Brief History of Fairfax County."
16. Sweig, "Brief History of Fairfax County."
17. *Fairfax Herald*, July 27, 1900.
18. Ravensworth Story, "Story of Ravensworth."
19. Dunn interview, 1971.
20. Shoop, *Place Called Ilda*, 6.
21. Dunn interview, 1971.
22. Glassell, Fairfax Deed Book, C-3, p. 42; Glassell, Fairfax Deed Book, F-3, p. 45.
23. Fairfax County History Commission, "Land Ownership."
24. Sweig, "Brief History of Fairfax County."
25. Hill interview, 2013.
26. Shoop, *Place Called Ilda*, 20–21.
27. Henderson, "Falls Church's Black History."
28. Robinson, "List of Blacks in Fairfax County."
29. Robinson, "List of Blacks in Fairfax County."
30. Robinson, "List of Blacks in Fairfax County."
31. U.S. Census 2023, *Merrifield VA-CDP*.
32. Kelly, "How Did Gallows Road Get Its Name?"
33. Kelly, "How Did Gallows Road Get Its Name?"
34. Kelly, "How Did Gallows Road Get Its Name?"
35. Kelly, "How Did Gallows Road Get Its Name?"
36. Tatevasion, "Merrifield Postmaster's Grandson Fights Fidel."
37. Dunn interview, 1971.
38. Dunn interview, 1971.
39. *Hopkins 1894 Map of Mills Crossing*, Ancestry.com.
40. Kelly, "How Did Gallows Road Get Its Name?"
41. Charles Coates, 1850, Ancestry.com.
42. Charles Coates, 1880, Ancestry.com.
43. Nimrod Dixon, "U.S., Freedmen's Bureau Records, 1865–1878, Ancestry.com.
44. Horace Gibson, Fairfax Deed Book, V-4, p. 434.
45. Robert Bradley, Fairfax Deed Book, D-5, p. 335–36.
46. Joshua Pearson, 1884, Fairfax Deed Book, S-5, Book 59.
47. First Baptist Church of Merrifield, Virginia, 1892, Fairfax Deed Book, N-5 p. 10.

48. George Harrison Tinner, Fairfax Deed Book, X-5, p. 41.
49. Historical Marker Database, "History of 'Gravel Bank.'"
50. Historical Marker Database, "History of 'Gravel Bank.'"
51. Wikipedia, "USS *Maine* (1889)."
52. Wikipedia, "USS *Maine* (1889)."
53. Swan, Historical Marker Data Base.
54. Shoop, *Place Called Ilda*.
55. Shoop, *Place Called Ilda*.
56. Viola Johnson-Richards, Northern Virginia Civil Rights Archive.
57. *Fairfax Herald* 49, no. 50 (May 1, 1931), via Virginia Chronicle.
58. Dunn interview, 1971.
59. Dunn interview, 1971.
60. Dunn interview, 1971.
61. Dunn interview, 1971.
62. Dunn interview, 1971.
63. Dunn interview, 1971.
64. Vincent's Garage and Service Station, Fairfax Trade Name Book 1, p. 188; Vincent's Hardware and Mercantile Store, Fairfax Trade Name Book 2, p. 85.
65. Harvey's Diner, Fairfax Trade Name Book, Book 3, p. 73.
66. Dunn interview, 1971.
67. Arnold, "German and United States Arnolds."
68. Jeff Bagato, "Garage D'Art: Johnston's Auto Paint and Body Works," www.panicresearch.com.
69. Bagato, "Garage D'Art."
70. Wright interview by Mary Lipsey.
71. Wright interview by Mary Lipsey.
72. Find-a-Grave, "George Alpheus Lyon Merrifield."
73. G.A.L. Merrifield, *Fairfax County Sun Echo*, April 19, 1962.
74. G.A.L. Merrifield, *Fairfax County Sun Echo*, April 19, 1962.
75. *Northern Virginia Sun* 22, no. 232 (July 2, 1959).
76. Whitmore interview by Nia King and Solenne Montgomery, March 6, 2021.
77. Naomi Zevin, "A Conversation with Four Women," Fairfax County History Commission, videotape, 2005.
78. Hill interview by Mary Lipsey.
79. Velma Johnson-Massenberg, Northern Virginia Civil Rights Archive, https://folklore.gmu.edu.
80. Massenberg, Northern Virginia Civil Rights Archive.

81. Massenberg, Northern Virginia Civil Rights Archive.

Chapter 3

82. Coleman, "How Literacy Became a Powerful Weapon."
83. Prasanna, "Frederick Douglass Learning to Read and Write Essay."
84. Brawley, *Social History of the American Negro*.
85. Freedmen's Bureau, "Summary of Census Returns."
86. Freedmen's Bureau, "Summary of Census Returns."
87. Gernand, *Virginia Village Goes to War*.
88. Taylor, *Negro in the Reconstruction of Virginia*.
89. Debbie Robison, Northern Virginia History Notes, https://novahistory.org.
90. Fairfax County Land Records, 1874 deed.
91. Fairfax County Land Records, 1884 deed.
92. Henderson, "Falls Church's Black History."
93. Bailey, "Census of School Population."
94. Bailey, "Census of School Population."
95. Hill interview, 2007.
96. Haight interview, 2007.
97. Fairfax County Public Schools, "School History: The Dunn Loring Elementary School."
98. Fairfax County Public Schools. "School History: James Lee Elementary School."
99. Fairfax County Public Schools. "School History: James Lee Elementary School."
100. Fairfax County Public Schools. "School History: James Lee Elementary School."
101. *Washington Post*, February 21, 1939, via ProQuest.
102. *Washington Post*, February 21, 1939, via ProQuest.
103. Hill interview, 2007.
104. Hill interview, 2007.
105. Keaney, "Long Road Toward Equity."

Chapter 4

106. Fairfax County Colored Citizens Association, *30th Anniversary Booklet*.
107. Fairfax County Colored Citizens Association, *30th Anniversary Booklet*.
108. Fairfax County Colored Citizens Association, *30th Anniversary Booklet*.

109. Fairfax County Colored Citizens Association, *30th Anniversary Booklet.*
110. Hill interview, 2013.

Chapter 5

111. Fairfax County Public School, Manassas Regional High School, https://jacksonms.fcps.edu/about/history/high.
112. Fairfax County School Board, "School History Sources, 1937–1965."
113. Haight interview, 2007.
114. Hill interview, 2007.

Chapter 6

115. Chicago Defender, "Hint Plots to Balk School Integration."
116. *Washington Post*, 1959.
117. *Washington Evening/Sunday Star*, 1961.
118. Fairfax County Public Schools, "FCPS by Numbers," https://www.fcps.edu/about-fcps
119. Fairfax County Public Schools, "FCPS by Numbers."

Chapter 7

120. Montgomery, *Under Their Own Vine and Fig Tree.*
121. Montgomery, *Under Their Own Vine and Fig Tree.*
122. Hill interview, 2007.
123. Fairfax County Deed Book R-4, page 320, Fairfax County Archives.
124. Andrew Gruman, Fairfax Deed Book, R-4, p. 320.
125. Margaret (Mary) Glassell, Fairfax Deed Book, C-3, p. 42.
126. Fairfax County History Commission, *1860 Fairfax County Map*, www.fairfaxcounty.gov.
127. Robert Bradley, Fairfax Deed Book, D-5, p. 335–36.
128. First Baptist Church of Merrifield, Fairfax Deed Book, N-5, p. 10.
129. First Baptist Church of Merrifield, Fairfax Deed Book, R-5, p. 127.
130. Hill interview, 2007.
131. Hill interview, 2013.
132. *Washington Bee*, November 1898.
133. *Fairfax Herald*, August 3, 1900.

134. As related by Reverend Herbin.
135. Historical Newspapers. *Washington Post*, June 22, 1929.
136. Du Bois, *The Negro*, 113–14.
137. Foner, *Reconstruction*.
138. Hill interview, 2007.

Chapter 8

139. Sons and Daughters of Liberty Lodge, Liber "F," no. 6, p. 188.
140. Charles Tinner, Fairfax Deed Book, X-5, 4.
141. Sacchi, *Pines and Liberty Lodge Cemetery*.
142. Sacchi, *Pines and Liberty Lodge Cemetery*.
143. Young, "Descendants Preserve Their Past."
144. Young, "Descendants Preserve Their Past."
145. Young, "Descendants Preserve Their Past."
146. Fairfax County Land Records, Deed Book P-7, page 476.
147. First Baptist Church of Merrifield, *100th Anniversary Book*, Merrifield, Virginia, 1994.
148. Hill interview, 2013.
149. *Fairfax Herald*, "Harrison Tinner," 5.
150. Grand United Order of Odd Fellows in America, records, 1911–46, Filson Historical Society.
151. Wikipedia, "Grand United Order of Odd Fellows in America."

Chapter 9

152. William H. Collins Jr., Fairfax Deed Book, X-6, p. 446.
153. Ancestry, "William H. Collin Sr."
154. Ancestry, "William H. Collin Sr."

Chapter 11

155. Karen King Ibrahim, Courtney Gaskins and Karen Hughes-White, *Fauquier County, Virginia Register of Free Negroes, 1817–1865*, archive.org.
156. Ibrahim, Gaskins and Hughes-White, *Fauquier County, Virginia Register of Free Negroes*.

157. Ibrahim, Gaskins and Hughes-White, *Fauquier County, Virginia Register of Free Negroes*.
158. Lucy Lee, U.S. Census, 1860, Ancestry.com.
159. James Lee, A.J. Chunn, Fauquier County Archives.
160. Crawford, "Uncommon Wealth."
161. Entrenchment letter, Fauquier County Courthouse, 1861, Afro American Museum in the Plains, Virginia.
162. Fairfax County Land Records, deed, James and Charles Lee, Fairfax County Courthouse no. 482-487, December 27, 1866.
163. Tinner Hill Heritage Foundation, http://tinnerhill.org/about/history.
164. Tinner Hill Heritage Foundation, http://tinnerhill.org/about/history.
165. Hill interview, 2013.
166. Steadman, *Falls Church*.
167. Second Baptist Church, Falls Church, Fairfax Land Deed—Trustees, 164–65.
168. Betsy Lee marriage letter, courtesy of Georgia Brown, Archivist, Fairfax County.

Chapter 12

169. Carter, "Official White House Letter."
170. Raboteau, *Canaan Land*, 43.
171. Raboteau, *Canaan Land*, 43.
172. James Edward Lee interview, February 4, 1919.
173. James Edward Lee interview, February 4, 1919.
174. Statement of Mr. George Thomas, Second Baptist Church Archives.
175. Thomas, statement, December 2, 1928.
176. James Edward Lee interview, February 4, 1919.
177. Carter, "Official White House Letter."
178. First Baptist Church of Warrenton, *One Hundred Year Anniversary Book*, Warrenton, Virginia, August 1967.
179. Fourteenth Annual Northern Virginia Baptist Association Session Minutes, Pleasant Grove Baptist Church, Orange County, Virginia, August 19–21, 1891, Afro American Museum.
180. Seventy-Fifth Annual Northern Virginia Baptist Association Session Minutes, August 1952, Afro-American Museum.
181. Fourteenth Annual Northern Virginia Baptist Association Session Minutes. The total membership listed in this minute book was 346 for

First Baptist of Warrenton—more than any other church assembled with the NVBA.
182. Lewis, *Undaunted Faith*, 5.
183. Seventy-Fifth Annual Northern Virginia Baptist Association Session Minutes, August 1952.
184. Seventy-Fifth Annual Northern Virginia Baptist Association Session Minutes, August 1952.
185. Northern Virginia Baptist Association, "Some Eventful Thoughts," 1967.
186. Fourteenth Annual Northern Virginia Baptist Association Session Minutes, August 19–21, 1891.
187. Fourteenth Annual Northern Virginia Baptist Association Session Minutes, August 19–21, 1891.
188. Montgomery, *Under Their Own Vine and Fig Tree*, 111.
189. Reverend Smith interview by Marion Dobbins, April 22, 2014.
190. Fourteenth Annual Northern Virginia Baptist Association Session Minutes, August 19–21, 1891, 17.
191. Fourteenth Annual Northern Virginia Baptist Association Session Minutes, August 19–21, 1891, 17.
192. Fourteenth Annual Northern Virginia Baptist Association Session Minutes, August 19–21, 1891, 17.
193. Hill interview, 2013.
194. Hill interview, 2013.
195. Hill interview, 2013.

Chapter 13

196. Jacqueline L. Salmon, "Park's Allure Hides Pain of Past," Washington Post, April 13, 2000.
197. Salmon, "Park's Allure Hides Pain of Past."
198. Salmon, "Park's Allure Hides Pain of Past."

Conclusion

199. James Edward Lee interview, February 4, 1919.
200. James Edward Lee interview, February 4, 1919.
201. *Richmond (VA) Planet*, April 30, 1904, via Library of Virginia.

BIBLIOGRAPHY

Afro-American Historical Association Database. https://www.aahafauquier.org/free-emancipated.

Ancestry. "1860 Federal Census for Mary R. Chichester." https://www.ancestry.com.

———. "J.H. Chichester Slave Schedule." https://www.ancestry.com.

———. "William H. Collin Sr." 1997. https://www.ancestry.com.

Arnold, Thelma. "German and United States Arnolds, 1455–1984." Family history.

Bailey, Ray T., District Clerk. "Census of School Population; District Clerk's Returns." Fairfax County Public School, 1890.

Brawley, Benjamin. *A Social History of the American Negro*. Macmillan Company, 1921.

Brundage, Fitzhugh W. *Lynching in the New South: Georgia and Virginia, 1880–1930*. University of Illinois Press, 1993.

Campbell, Marilyn. "Uncovering the Roots of Slavery." *Connection*, February 16, 2016. https://www.connectionnewspapers.com/news/2016/feb/16/uncovering-roots-slavery.

Carter, Jimmy. "Official White House Letter of Acknowledgment 100th Anniversary of the NVBA." Washington, D.C., August 22, 1977.

Chicago Defender. "Hint Plots to Balk School Integration." 1953. https://www.fcps.edu/about-fcps/history/records/desegregation/newspapers.

Coleman, Colette. "How Literacy Became a Powerful Weapon in the Fight to End Slavery." History, June 22, 2024. https://www.history.com/news/nat-turner-rebellion-literacy-slavery.

Crawford, Greg, State Archivist. "The Uncommon Wealth: The Voices from the Library of Virginia." Library of Virginia. https://uncommonwealth.virginiamemory.com/blog/2016/01/20/virginia-untold-requisitions-for-public-use.

Department of Commerce, Bureau of Public Roads. National Archives. April 1, 1967. https://catalog.archives.gov/search?q=Fairfax%20county%20virginia.

Du Bois, W.E.B. *The Negro*. Reprint. Oxford University Press, 1970.

Dunn, Pearl. Interview by Steve Matthews. *Echoes of History* 4 (August 20, 1971).

Fairfax County Administration. "Mr. G.A.L. Merrifield." Letter to Mrs. Lois Gullette. Springfield, Virginia, February 3, 1983.

Fairfax County Colored Citizens Association. *30th Anniversary Booklet.* https://www.fairfaxcounty.gov/history-commission/sites/history-commission/files/assets/documents/aahi/30th-anniversary-booklet.pdf.

Fairfax County Historical Society. 2023. https://fairfaxhistoricalsociety.org.

Fairfax County History Commission. "Land Ownership in Fairfax County in 1860." 1988. https://www.fairfaxcounty.gov/history-commission/sites/history-commission/files/Assets/documents/1860CountyMap/49-4.jpg.

Fairfax County Land Records. 1884 Deed of Purchase. Fairfax Deed Book D-5:362.

———. 1874 Deed of Purchase. Fairfax Deed Book R-4:439.

Fairfax County Public Schools. "School History: James Lee Elementary School." 2024. https://www.fcps.edu/about-fcps/history/records/desegregation/schools/james-lee.

———. "School History: The Dunn Loring Elementary School." 2024. https://www.fcps.edu/about-fcps/history/closed/dunn-loring.

Fairfax County School Board. "School History Sources, 1937–1965." https://jacksonms.fcps.edu/about/history/high/sources#:~:text=January%205,%201952,%20Page.

Fairfax Herald. August 3, 1900. Via Virginia Chronicle, Library of Virginia. https://virginiachronicle.com.

———. "Harrison Tinner, Member of the Road Improvement Group." September 9, 1927, 5.

———. July 27, 1900. Via Virginia Chronicle. https://virginiachronicle.com.

Foner, Eric. *Reconstruction: America's Unfinished Revolution, 1863–1877.* HarperCollins, 2005.

Fourth Estate. "Mason Student Explores the History of Slaves in Fairfax County." November 18, 2015. https://gmufourthestate.com/2015/11/18/mason-student-explores-the-history-of-slaves-in-fairfax-county.

Freedmen's Bureau. "Summary of Census Returns of Colored People, Fairfax County, Virginia, November 15th, 1865." Available online.

Gernand, Bradley. *A Virginia Village Goes to War: Falls Church During the Civil War*. Donning Company for the Village Preservation and Improvement Society of Falls Church, 2002.

Grand United Order of Odd Fellows in America. Records, 1911–46. Filson Historical Society.

Haight, Helen. Interview by Mary Lipsey, September 28, 2007.

Hardy, Tanya Gaskins. *Standin' On Faith: The Story of Galloway United Methodist Church*. United Methodist Church, 2011.

Henderson, Edwin B., II. "Falls Church's Black History: A Welcoming Community that Has Not Always Been So Welcoming." *Falls Church's Pulse*, February 15, 2024. https://fallschurchpulse.org/falls-churchs-black-history-henderson.

Hill, Avonjeannette. Interviewed by Marion Dobbins, Annandale, Virginia, September 20, 2013. Civil Rights Archives, Library of Congress.

Hill, Avonjeantte ("Dolly"). Interview by Mary Lipsey, November 28, 2007.

Historical Marker Database. "History of 'Gravel Bank.'" 2021. HMdb.org.

Historical Newspapers. *Washington Post*, June 22, 1929. Via ProQuest. https://www.proquest.com/docview/150006812/fulltextPDF/5364B62823AE4DA6PQ/1?accountid=14541&sourcetype=Historical%20Newspapers.

Hopkins, G.M. *Hopkins 1894 Map of Mills Crossing*. Virginia Places. http://virginiaplaces.org/vacount/graphics/merrifield1894.png.

Keaney, Maura. "Long Road Toward Equity: Segregation and Desegregation in Fairfax County, Virginia Schools." December 2019. https://sites.google.com/view/fcps-desegregation/home.

Kelly, John. "How Did Gallows Road Get Its Name?" *Washington Post*, November 14, 2014. https://www.washingtonpost.com/local/how-did-gallows-road-get-its-name/2014/11/22/cb07148e-7183-11e4-ad12-3734c461eab6_story.html.

Lee, James Edward. Interview, taken from the Second Baptist Church's Old Church records, February 4, 1919.

Lewis, Stephen Johnson. *Undaunted Faith: The Story of Jennie Dean*. Manassas Museum System, 1994.

Montgomery, William E. *Under Their Own Vine and Fig Tree: The African American Church in the South, 1865–1900*. Louisiana State University Press, 1993.

Northern Virginia History Notes. "Educating Freedmen During Reconstruction in Fairfax County." December 6, 2014. https://www.novahistory.org/FreedmenEducation/FreedmenEducation.htm.

Northern Virginia Sun 22, no. 232 (July 2, 1959). https://virginiachronicle.com.

Oberle, George. "Total Population of Fairfax County by Race, 1860–1970." https://georgeoberle.org/historicmarkers/files/original/5ffec5d639ce1d82cc16ebc951035a25.pdf.

Pargas, Damian Alan. *The Quarters and the Fields: Slave Families in the Non-Cotton South*. University Press of Florida, 2010.

Porter, Robert. "Letter to Mr. H.H. Douglas, Executive Director." 1971.

Prasanna. "Frederick Douglass Learning to Read and Write Essay." June 8, 2021. https://www.aplustopper.com/frederick-douglass-learning-to-read-and-write-essay.

Raboteau, Albert J. *Canaan Land: A Religious History of African Americans*. Oxford University Press, 1999.

The Ravensworth Story: A History of the Ravensworth Landgrant in Fairfax County, Virginia. "The Story of Ravensworth: Paynes Mill/Rock Hill." 2024. https://ravensworthstory.org/landmarks/paynes-mill-rock-hill.

Robinson, Debbie. "List of Blacks in Fairfax County, 1866–1869." Northern Virginia History Notes, June 2, 2017. https://www.novahistory.org/Fairfax_Blacks_1866-1869/Fairfax_Blacks_1866-1869.htm.

Sacchi, Richard. *The Pines and Liberty Lodge Cemetery*. Fairfax County Park Authority, 2001.

Second Baptist Church. "The History of Second Baptist." 2018. https://sbcfallschurch.org/history.

Shoop, Tom. *A Place Called Ilda*. University of Virginia Press, 2024.

Shuman, Sue Kovach. *Mantua*. Images of America Series. Arcadia Publishing, 2021.

Smith, Reverend Kenny, DD. Interview by Marion Dobbins, Prince William County, Virginia, April 22, 2014.

Steadman, Melvin Lee. *Falls Church: Fence and Fire*. Turnpike Press, 1964.

Swan, Craig. Historical Marker Data Base. June 17, 2023. https://www.hmdb.org/m.asp?m=4183.

Sweig, Donald, PhD. "A Brief History of Fairfax County." https://www.fairfaxcounty.gov/planning-development/sites/planning-development/files/assets/documents/historic/history275.pdf.

———. "A Short History of Fairfax County." https://www.fairfaxcounty.gov/planning-development/sites/planning-development/files/assets/documents/historic/history275.pdf.

Tatevasion, Roosevelt Der. "Merrifield Postmaster's Grandson Fights Fidel." *Fairfax County Sun Echo*, 1962.

Taylor, Alrutheus Ambush, AM. *The Negro in the Reconstruction of Virginia*. Atheneum Publishers Inc., 1926.

Terry, Aaron. Interviewed by Marion Dobbins, Arlington, Virginia, October 30, 2013. Civil Rights Archives, Library of Congress.

Thomas, George. Statement, December 2, 1928. Second Baptist Archives.

U.S. Census 2023. *Merrifield VA-CDP*. https://www.census.gov/quickfacts/fact/dashboard/merrifieldcdpvirginia,medfieldcdpmassachusetts/PST045223.

Washington Evening/Sunday Star. January 25, 1961. https://www.fcps.edu/about-fcps/history/records/desegregation/newspapers#washington-star.

Washington Post. "Fairfax County Public Schools." May 21, 1954. https://www.fcps.edu/about-fcps/history/records/desegregation/newspapers#washington-post.

———. "Washington Post Historical Papers." February 21, 1939. Via ProQuest. https://www.proquest.com/hnpwashingtonpost/docview/151206431/2604F6E754304A53PQ/23?accountid=34227&sourcetype=Historical%20Newspapers.

Whitmore, Robert (Bobbi) Gibbs. Interview by Nia King and Solenne Montgomery, March 6, 2021.

Wikipedia. "Grand United Order of Odd Fellows in America." December 19, 2024. https://en.wikipedia.org/wiki/Grand_United_Order_of_Odd_Fellows_in_America.

———. "USS *Maine* (1889)." July 14, 2024. https://en.wikipedia.org/wiki/USS_Maine_(1889).

Wright, Aileen. Interview by Mary Lipsey, October 25, 2007. Providence District History Project Providence Perspective.

Young, Cynthia F. "Descendants Preserve Their Past; Merrifield Cemetery Is Restored." *Fairfax Journal*, 1998.

Zeavin, Naomi Sokol, and Fairfax County History Commission. *African American History in Mason District*. Fairfax County History Commission, 2005.

ABOUT THE AUTHOR

Marion Ransell Dobbins was born and raised in Merrifield. From a young age, she was drawn to history. As a child, she sat at her grandmother's knee and listened to the stories of her ancestors and the communities they built. However, from the 1960s to the 1980s, Marion became disheartened by the changing landscape of the Black communities and the growing disregard for their historical significance. Over the past four decades, she has dedicated herself to researching, collecting and speaking out about these lost spaces in Merrifield, the Pines and Williamstown and the people who built them. Marion is currently a community historian at George Mason University for the Center for Mason Legacy and is currently working to complete her PhD in American and African American history.